MAKING METRIC MANEUVERS

A RESOURCE GUIDE

Mary Richardson Miller
Classroom Teacher, Grades 1-6, 9-12
Mathematics Committee Chairman
Belmont School District
Belmont, California

Toni Cresswell Richardson
Resource Teacher, K-6
Staff Development Committee
Belmont School District
Belmont, California

ACTIVITY RESOURCES COMPANY
P.O. Box 4875
Hayward, California 94545

Typeset by Vera Allen Composition - Cover Design, Betty Leister.

To that meticulous man
Approximately two meters tall,
And weighing about 100 Kilograms,
100 Kilos of HEART -
All HEART of pure gold!

Mr. Howard F. Kraus
Instructional Designer
Belmont School District
Belmont, California

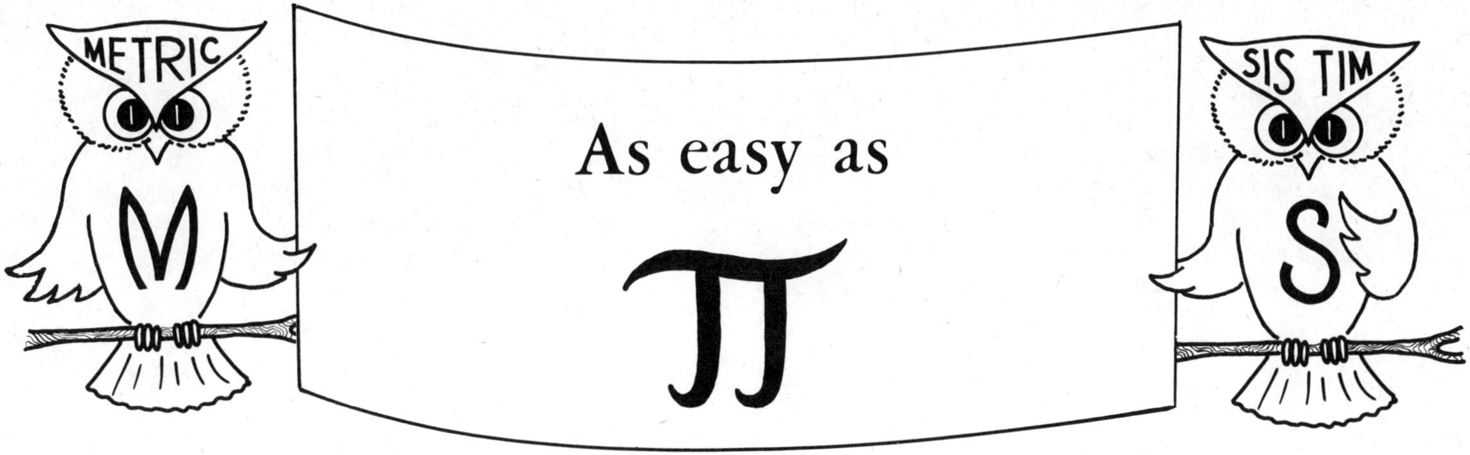

As classroom teachers, the authors of "Making Metric Maneuvers" have great respect for other classroom teachers who will successfully implement the Metric System in their own classrooms, despite the fact that many will have to learn metrics. Competent teachers will have no difficulty learning metrics. The authors also realize that classroom teachers are constantly meeting new demands and assuming increased responsibilities. Some may have no time to make extensive preparations for an effective implementation of the Metric System of Weights and Measures. Therefore, this resource guide was prepared for teachers who want or need help. It was also prepared for teachers who want to save time for developing special interests. However, the most important reason for preparing this guide was to give pupils opportunities to enjoy the introduction of the metric system through activities which Nesbit School pupils enjoyed. "Making Metric Maneuvers" includes aids for teachers in addition to the classroom-tested and revised activities.

General Overview

What is "Making Metric Manuevers"?

"Making Metric Maneuvers" is a Resource Guide to help teachers implement Metrics within classrooms. This guide provides aids prepared for efficient and effective implementation of the Metric System of Weights and Measures.

What is the objective?

These activities introduce pupils to the Metric System of Weights and Measures. They provide a challenging and enjoyable introduction in understanding and using Metrics. To encourage extensions, many activities are open-ended.

What aids are provided for classroom teachers?

Information necessary for introducing Metrics Activities for pupils printed on activity pages designed for reproduction as Task Cards or Activity Sheets for use within a classroom. A classroom teacher may wish to consider these suggestions:

1. A page may be removed from the guide and used at a Learning Center or on a Bulletin Board as an aid or a motivating device.

2. Illustrations may be cut out and used. For instance, the large pictures of the owls (see appendix) may be colored, cut out and used in setting up a Bulletin Board or a Learning Center.
3. Pages may be duplicated on transparencies for various uses in a classroom.
4. Pages may be reproduced in any available copying machine, or made into ditto sheets and reproduced for classroom use: with the total class, with large and small groups, for flexible grouping, in a learning center, as a worksheet, for individual investigation.

What kinds of student activities?

Group cooperation and the big muscle activities of running, reaching, measuring, and recording make use of the school environment for learning.

Organization

The guide is divided into

1. Linear
2. Area
3. Capacity
4. Mass
5. Temperature
6. Appendix

Table of Contents

LINEAR

Whoo School Owl Race

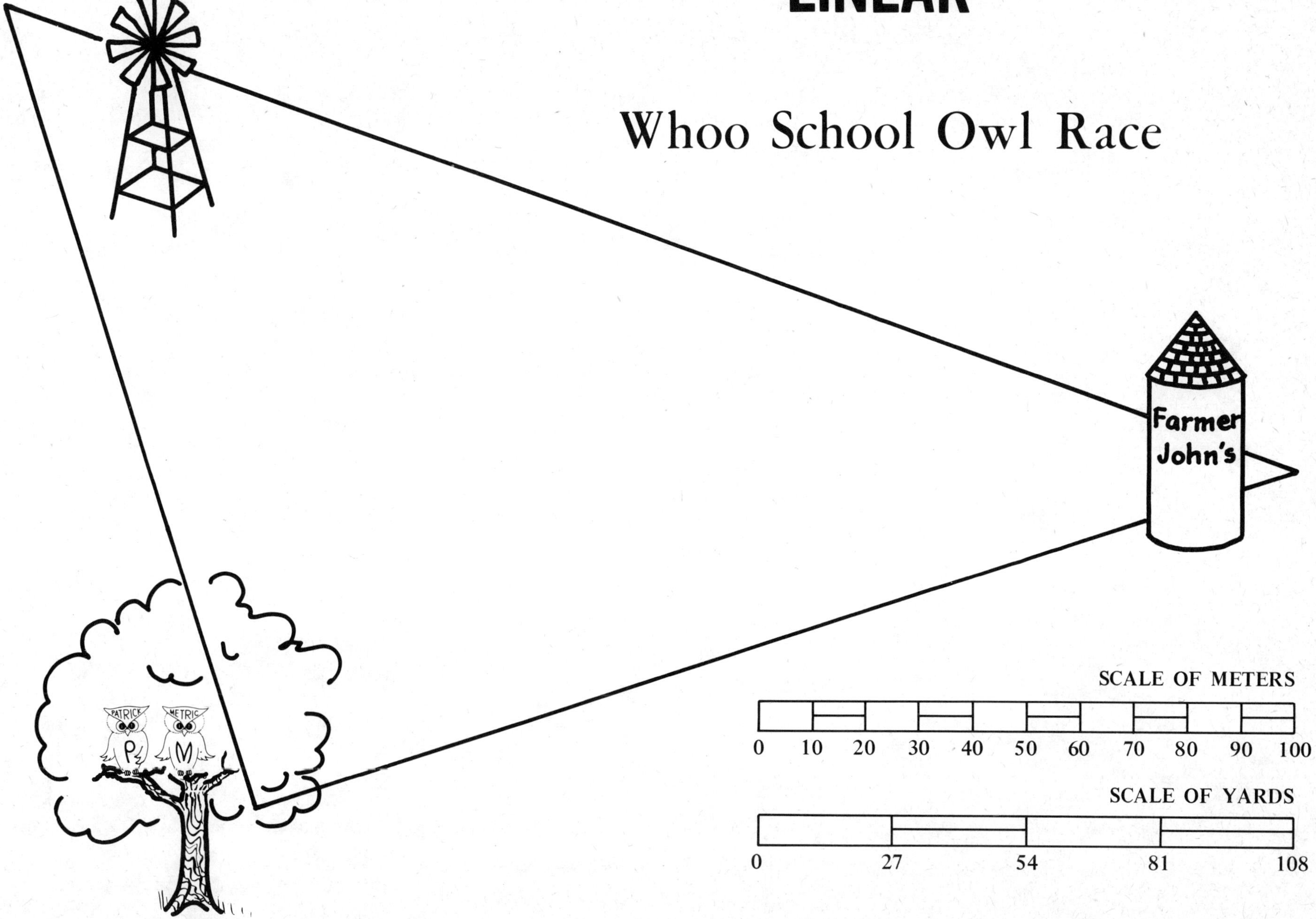

Whoo School Owl Race Story

(For the teacher to tell, read, or record on tape to be played back by students.)

All the owls began gathering for the Whoo School Owl Race. Two owls were racing. Patrick and Metric. They perched at the starting line in the old oak tree. The wisest owl, Sis Tim, flew in to signal the start of the race. She raised her wing and signalled. Patrick and Metric zoomed off. Beak to beak they flew.

All the other owls sat in the old oak tree. The older owls cheered. The little owls watched.

Patrick and Metric flew toward the first marker. Still beak to beak! Around Farmer John's silo they swooped. Patrick sped ahead. Metric trailed. Toward the windmill they flew. Metric began gaining. Patrick seemed to be getting tired. He faltered. Metric lurched ahead, and rounded the windmill first. Metric flapped his wings. He soared. Patrick tailed Metric. Beak to beak again! Patrick and Metric zoomed toward the old oak tree.

Which owl do you think will win? Raise your left hand if you think Patrick will win. Raise your right hand if you think Metric will win.

Half of the little owls sitting in the old oak tree cheered for Patrick and the other half of the little owls cheered for Metric. The little owls flapped their wings. One almost tumbled off a branch. He screeched. Sis Tim caught him in time. The little owl spotted Patrick and flapped his wings again.

Patrick and Metric neared the finish line. Metric landed in the oak tree. So did Patrick. Metric won the race.

The little owls rushed toward Metric and Patrick. All the little owls hopped up and down around Metric. Sis Tim stepped forward. She looked at Patrick.

"Patrick!" she began, "How far did you fly?" Patrick tried to add the distance in his head. Finally, he grabbed a twig and began making marks on the bark of the oak tree.

"656 yards," he answered.

"656 yards"" repeated Sis Tim. The little owl, who had almost fallen off a branch, began flapping his wings and hooting.

"656 yards isn't right," he hooted. "I measured 656 yards three and nine sixteenths inches."

"Your measurement *is* more precise, "Sis Tim said gently. "But 656 yards to the nearest yard is the more accurate measurement." The little owl ruffled his feathers.

"B-b-but," he stammered, "656 yards is only an approximate measurement." The little owl flapped his wings. He almost tumbled off the branch again. This time he regained his balance without Sis Tim's help. She stepped toward him. Shaking her wise head, she paused and stood tall.

"656 yards is an approximate number," she explained. "All measurements are stated in approximate numbers. Didn't you know that?"

The little owl lowered his eyes. He did not answer. The other little owls sat motionless. They waited for Sis Tim to say something. She wrapped her wing around the little owl.

"656 yards is a better answer than yours because it is accurate enough for our purposes and easier to work with than the more exact number," she said.

"How far did you fly, Metric?" she asked.

"600 meters," Metric replied. The little owls chattered among themselves. The older owls watched and listened. They nodded in understanding. One brave little owl questioningly raised her wing.

"How could Patrick and Metric fly the same race and have different answers?" she asked. Her eyes sparkled. She gazed at Sis Tim. Sis Tim looked around. All the owls sat waiting for her answer. Sis Tim puffed out her chest.

"We have several different systems of measurement," she

said. Nodding toward Patrick, Sis Tim continued, "Patrick gave his answer in a unit of the English System of Measures." Sis Tim nodded at Metric and spoke, "Metric gave his answer in a unit of the Metric System." The other little owls twitched and looked puzzled.

Sis Tim continued in a wise tone, "Patrick measured in yards and Metric measured in meters."

"Tell us more," begged the little owls. Sis Tim lifted her gaze to the owls perched in the oak.

"In 1790," she said, "Thomas Jefferson started to develop a system of measures." Patrick raised his wing.

"Who was Thomas Jefferson?" he asked. Metric gulped.

"Don't you know who Thomas Jefferson was?" Metric asked Patrick. "Thomas Jefferson lived during the time of Patrick Henry. You must know Patrick Henry."

"Yes, but I want to know who Thomas Jefferson was!" Patrick turned toward Sis Tim and waited for her answer. She shifted from one leg to the other.

"Thomas Jefferson," Sis Tim began. She paused, shifted a leg and said, "Thomas Jefferson was one of the founding fathers of our country. In 1790, he was Secretary of State." Sis Tim looked at Patrick. He seemed satisfied so she continued, "Thomas Jefferson wanted a system of measures that followed a ratio of 1 to 10. That means that adjacent orders of a system of measures would be 1 to 10 or 10 to 1. All of the orders would be in powers of ten as in our decimal notation. In fact, all of the multiples and subdivisions of a standard unit could be divided by ten." The little owls flapped their wings.

One little owl screeched. "That means we wouldn't have to multiply or divide by 12, or 3, or 36, or 5½, or 16, or 4 or any other number to change one kind of units to another," the little owl said hurriedly. "And we wouldn't have to learn fractions like 1/8, 4/5, 1/3, 3/16 and all the others. We could use decimals!" The little owl gasped for breath and spoke to Sis Tim, "Tell us more!"

Sis Tim resumed her lesson. "Thomas Jefferson wanted a standard unit of measure that never changed. He wanted all the units of length, capacity and weight directly related to each other. He wanted a decimal system like our money system." Patrick flapped his wings.

"Oh," he said. "You mean like the dime and the dollar?" Sis Tim nodded in approval.

"Yes, Patrick, like the dime and the dollar." Sis Tim took a deep breath. "Thomas Jefferson proposed that in 1790. In the very same year, a group of scientists in France met at the Academy of Science in Paris. They developed a system of weights and measures similar to the one Thomas Jefferson wanted." Sis Tim's eyes sparkled as she continued, "These scientists decided to use the Greek word *meter* for the basic unit of length. By definition, the distance between two marks on a platinum bar became the distance of a meter. Their decimal system was based on science and logic. The orders were related in a 1 to 10 or a 10 to 1 ratio. Their system of weights and measures became known as the "Metric System." Sis Tim paused.

"Can anyone tell me where Metric got his name?" she asked. Patrick jumped up before the other owls could lift an eyelash. He puffed out his chest.

"Metric was named after the Metric System of Weights and Measures," he said excitedly. "Now I know why his race was measured in meters. Can I learn to measure in meters?" Sis Tim nodded.

"All of us can learn to measure in meters."

Step it Off

Set up the course for the owls' race. Measure the course by counting the paces you need to walk the course. _______number of paces.

Measure a string by walking the same number of paces on it. Cut the string and use it to measure the owls' course again. Does the length of the string match the length of the course?

Compare your string with those of others. Are all the strings the same length? Explain.

Pace the Race

Select a Partner

One will measure the distance of the owls' race in yards.________ yards (yds.)

One will use a meter stick to measure the same distance in meters.________ meters (m).

Did both of you get the same number of units? Is the distance both of you measured the same length?______________ Did you use the same units?______________

Run a race with your partner.
Run the distance you measured.

*Use a stop watch to measure the time of each. How many meters per second did each of you run?

Run a Race

Your teacher or an aid will set up the owls' race course on the playground for you.

Use a string to measure the distance of the race course. Cut the string and use it to measure the distance of a new race course. Make your distance a straight line for your course.

Run a race with someone on your new course.

*Use a stop watch to measure the time of each. Compare the distances in meters per second.

Compare

Look at the page with the diagram of the Owl Race. Find the key that shows you the scale for a meter and the scale for a yard.

Use the scales to find the distance Patrick and Metric flew.

Distance in yards __________

Distance in meters__________

Is the number of yards the same as the number of meters?

Explain.

From Races to Paces

Set up the owls' race course in an auditorium or on the playground. Use labelled boxes for the tree, the silo and the windmill.

Walk the race course and count your paces. Record the number of your paces.
______ paces.

COMPARE RESULTS: Compare the number of paces you counted with the number of paces others counted.

Did everyone measure the same distance?

Did everyone count the same number of paces?

Why or why not?

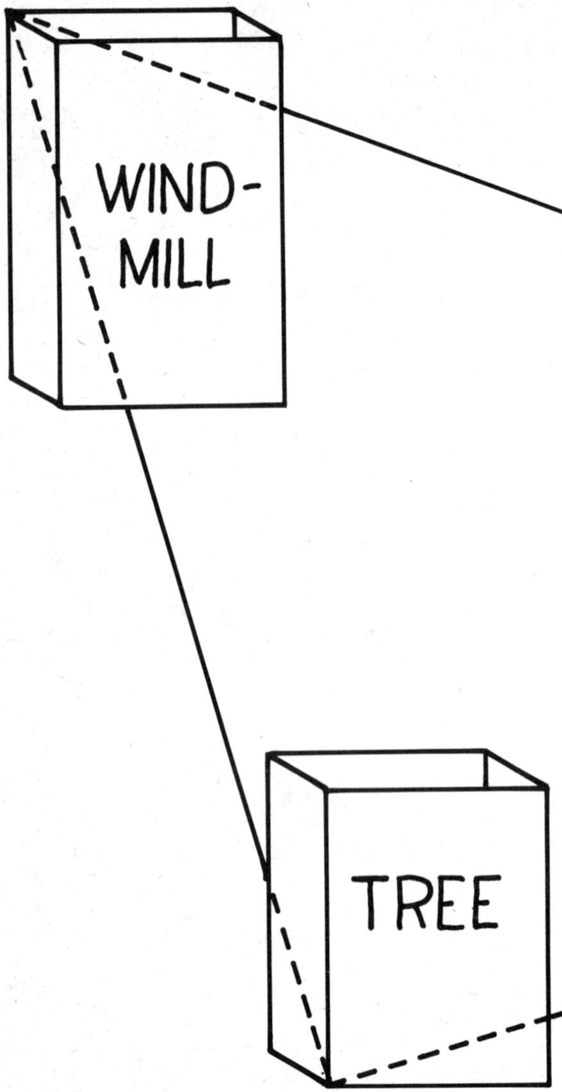

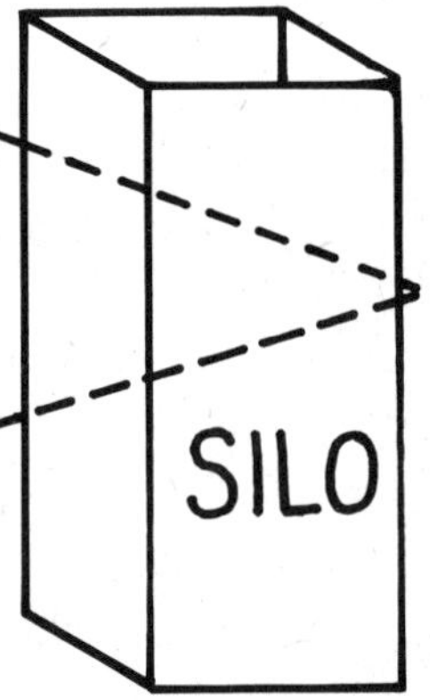

A pace is a step.

Windmill

A Race Course

Set up a small race course for the owls in your classroom. Write labels for the tree, silo and windmill. Put a label at each angle of an imaginary triangle.

Measure the distance of your race course by counting your paces as you walk around the course. ______ number of paces.

Silo

Use the number of paces you counted for the number of finger-lengths you will use to measure a strip of adding machine tape. Use the length of your index finger to measure the tape in finger-lengths. Cut the tape. Write the number of finger-lengths on the tape.

Tree

Of course!

Compare results with others.

Finger Length

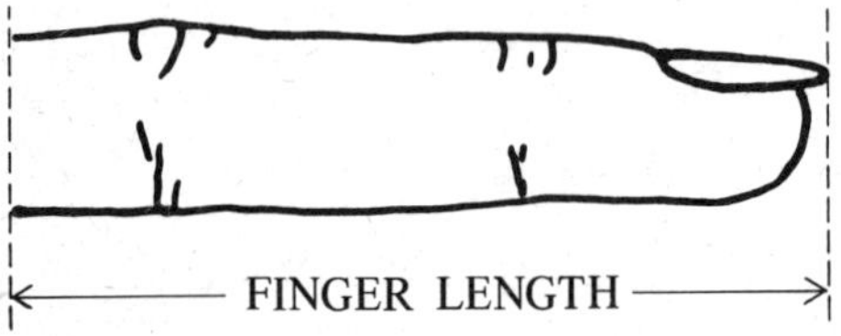

Use a finger-length as a unit to measure 20 finger-lengths of adding machine tape. Cut off the 20 unit length and put it on the front wall.

Use a finger-width as a unit to measure 40 finger-widths of adding machine tape. Cut off the 40 unit length and put it on a side wall.

Compare the length of your tapes with the lengths of tapes other pupils measured and put up on walls.

How do you account for the differences in the lengths of the tapes?

How can we select one of the lengths of tape as a standard unit for our class?

*Could we use the mean, average or median tape?

Our Standard Unit

How could our class select and define a standard unit of linear measures?

Any class can adopt a standard unit by definition.

What are the advantages?
What are the disadvantages?

Any country can also define and adopt a standard unit. So can any state in our country.

Then why have most countries adopted the international meter as a standard of length?

Metric Table

Linear Measurements

1 myriameter	=	10,000 meters
1 kilometer	=	1,000 meters
1 hectometer	=	100 meters
1 decameter	=	10 meters
1 meter	=	1 meter
1 decimeter	=	.1 meter
1 centimeter	=	.01 meter
1 millimeter	=	.001 meter

Therefore:

10 decimeters	=	1 meter
100 centimeters	=	1 meter
1000 millimeters	=	1 meter

S-t-r-i-n-g-i-n-g along with a Meter

How long do you think a meter is?

Patrick doesn't know, but he wants to know. Let's help Patrick.

1 dm

This is a decimeter unit. Cut it out.
Use your decimeter unit to measure a string 10 dm long.
10 decimeters measure the length of a meter (m).
Cut a string 1 meter (10 decimeters) long.
Check the length of your meter string with a meter stick.
Use your string to measure objects like doors.
Measure the length and width of your classroom.

Maneuvering Around Your School

Use your meter string or a meter stick to find these distances from your classroom to:

the auditorium or cafeteria
the library
the school office
the nearest restroom
the nearest fire alarm
the playground
the best drinking fountain
the route for your fire drill

*Draw a floor plan of your school.
Let 1 decimeter stand for 100 meters (1 Hectometer).

Junior Olympics

Every year pupils at Nesbit School in Belmont, California, run races in Junior Olympics held on their playground. Could you mark the distances of these races for them?

30 Meter Sack Race
50 Meter Dash
100 Meter Relay

Use your Meter string or a Meter stick to find the distances on your playground. Mark the distance of each race. Run the races with your friends.

*Find your time per meter and your distance per second for each race. Show your data on a bar graph.

A decimeter (dm)

What is a Meter?

Let's find out!

Use a decimeter to measure a strip of tagboard 10 dm long and 1 dm wide. Cut out the strip.

How long is a meter (m)? It is 10____________.

Is a meter about as long as your foot, arm or leg? Use your meter tagboard to find objects about **a meter** long.

*Divide your meter into 10 units of equal length.

What is the name of each of the 10 units?____________

The Latin prefix "deci-" means one tenth. We write 1/10 like this: .1

A________ is .1 of a meter. A meter is equivalent to ________dm.

Measurements Around You

Guess the measurements of these things:	Estimates	Measurements
Length of your desk	________ dm.	________ dm.
Height of your desk	________ dm.	________ dm.
Length of your reading book	________ dm.	________ dm.
Height of a wastepaper basket	________ dm.	________ dm.
Width of a magazine	________ dm.	________ dm.
Width of the sink	________ dm.	________ dm.

Write your guesses (estimates) in decimeters.

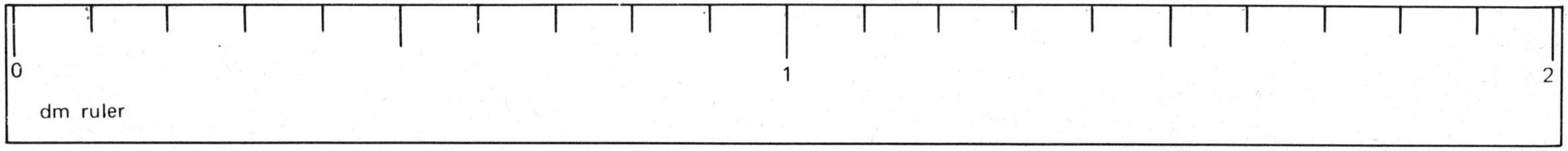

Cut out this decimeter ruler. Use it to measure the above things. Compare your measurements with your estimates and a red line for your measurements. Use cm. grid paper.

Use Your Metric Ruler

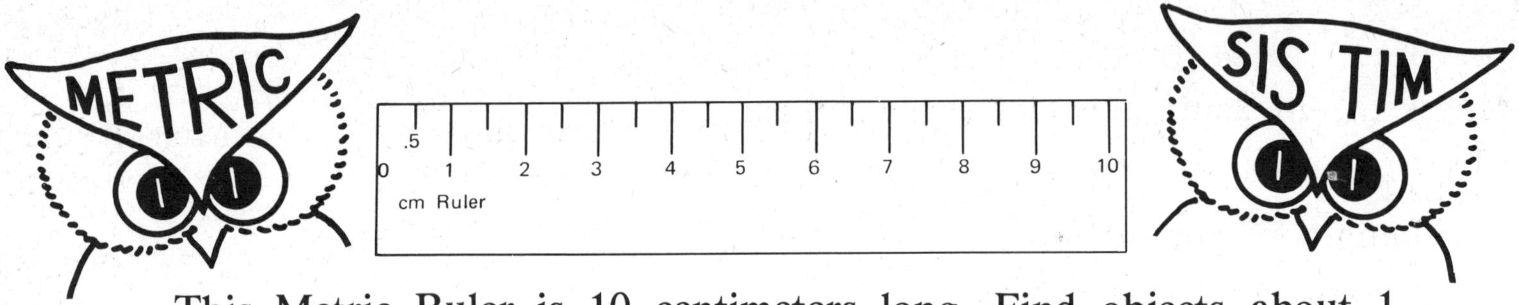

This Metric Ruler is 10 centimeters long. Find objects about 1 centimeter long. Write the names.

About how wide is your little finger?_____ cm

Write the names of objects about 5 cm long.

Measure a paper clip in centimeters. It is_______cm long.

Measure objects about 10 cm long.

Record the number of centimeters for each length.

Draw a line to show each length.

Draw a line 1 dm long. Find objects about 1 dm long.

*Mark the centimeters on a tagboard meter. Count the cm.

The Latin prefix "centi-" means one hundredth. 1/100 = .01.

Thumb Thumb

How many times do you think the width of your thumb will go across the top of this page? __________

Check your guess by measuring with your thumb. Number of thumb-widths __________

Use your thumb-width as a unit of measure to find the lengths of:

your nose _____ the palm of your hand _____ your mouth _____

How does your thumb-width compare with a centimeter (cm)?

Make your thumb print in the above box. Measure the print in cm.

Do you think your thumb would be useful for making estimates? Why?

*Use your data to find the distance across the top of the page. _____ cm

Use a metric ruler to check the length of this page. _____ cm

Compare your two measurements. Which is more accurate? Why?

*Why do people estimate distances?

Use your thumb: estimate more lengths.

Figuring Fingers

How wide do you think you index finger is? Measure it in cm_____cm

Which one of your fingers has a width nearest one centimeter?

Use that finger-width to estimate widths of many small objects and a desk.

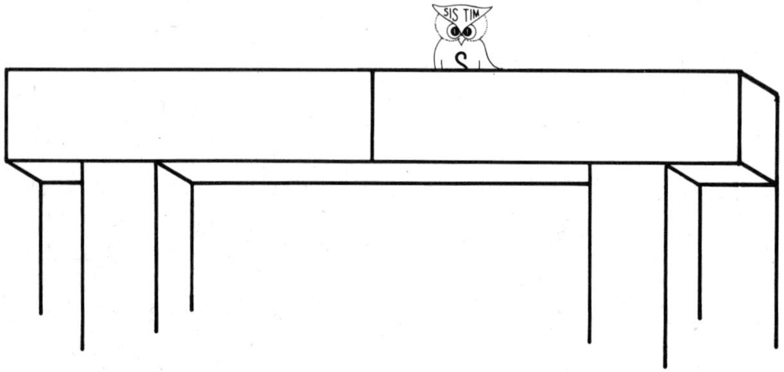

How Tall Are You?

Cut a strip of paper 1 dm by 2 m long. Stick it up on a wall. Check to be certain that the bottom of the strip touches the floor. Let a classmate mark your height. Cut the strip at your height. Measure the strip in centimeters (cm).

At the top of your strip write the number of cm and your name. Hang your strip up on the wall in your classroom.

How tall are you?

I am ______ centimeters tall.

I am ______ millimeters tall.

I am ______ meters tall.

I am ______ kilometers tall.

I am ______ decimeters tall.

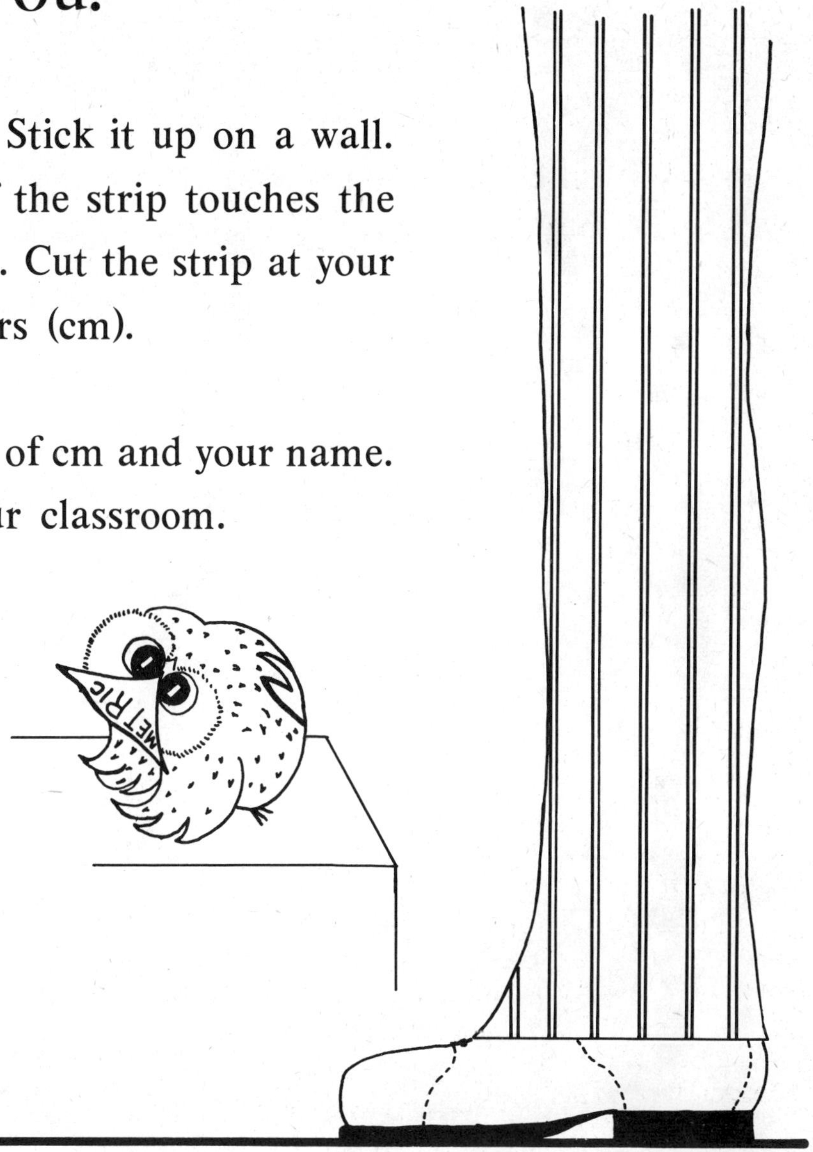

Let's Compare

Find the strip of paper that measured the tallest pupil in your room. Put that strip up on the wall.

Put up on the wall in order all the strips of paper that measured heights. Put up the strips to show heights from the tallest to the shortest.

What could you call these strips of paper ordering heights from the tallest to the shortest pupil? ________________________________

Yes, you have made a bar graph.
It is a simple bar graph.

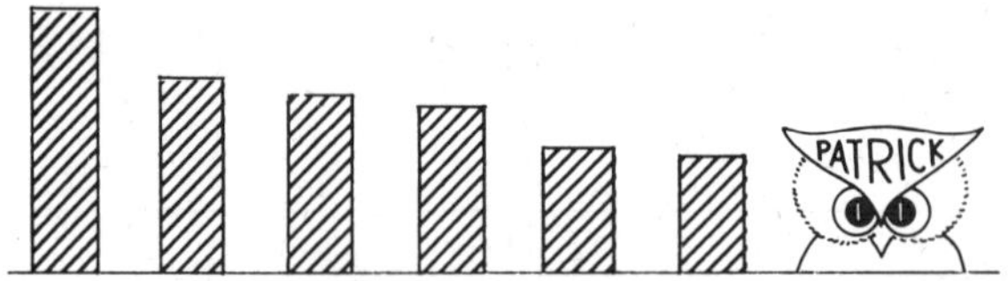

Make a bar graph on centimeter paper to show the ordering of these heights.

*What is the average height in this class?______cm. What is the mean?
*What per cent of the heights are above the average height in this class?

Shadow Measurement

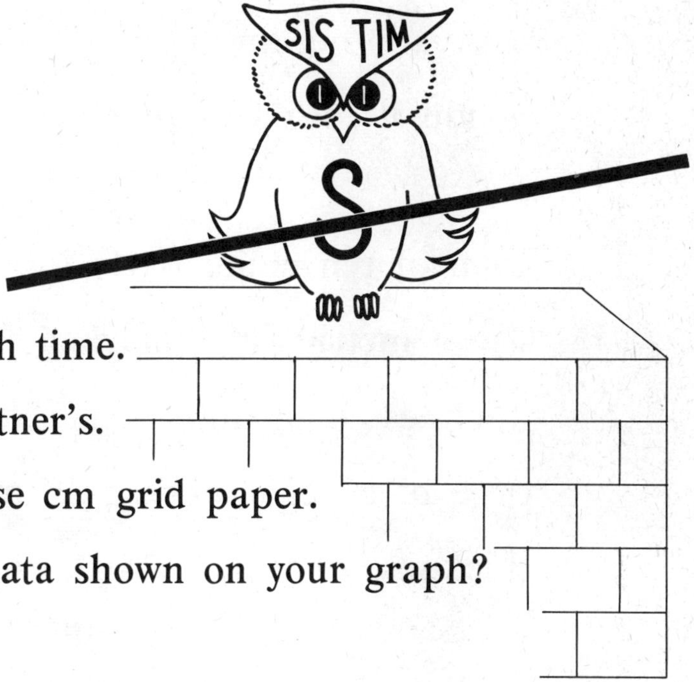

Get a partner.

Measure your shadows every hour.

Be sure you stand in the same place each time.

Record your measurements and your partner's.

Make a graph to show the difference. Use cm grid paper.

What conclusions have you made from data shown on your graph?

*How many cm tall are you?_____ cm.

Then how many meters tall are you?_______ m

Measure your shadow again. Record the length in meters._____ m

At this same time measure in length of a shadow cast by your school building. Record the length in meters._____ m

Use your data to find the approximate height of your school building.

Meet Milli-

Without using a cm ruler, draw a line 1 cm long.

Use a cm ruler to check the length of your line.

Draw another line 1 cm long.

Divide it into 10 equal parts.

Each of ten equal parts in a centimeter is called a millimeter (mm).

Use a metric ruler marked in mm to measure these tiny things:

thickness of a dime ____mm	width of a paper clip ____ mm
edge of a sugar cube ____mm	thickness of a half dollar ____ mm
thickness of a nickel ____ mm	height of a stack of 10 dimes ____ mm

width of the fingernail on your little finger _____ mm

width (diameter) of a soda straw _____ mm

Which measurement was approximately 1 mm? Circle it orange.

*Find objects with dimensions $<$ 10 mm.

Carefully make measurements in mm.

Rooting for You

On the left side of the grid divide each cm of the dark line into mm.

Number the mm's by 10's. Start at 30.

On the bottom of the grid number the weeks. Start at 3.

Cut off the stems and leaves of a carrot. Cut off the top of the carrot. Put the carrot top in a jar lid. Fill the lid with water. Put fresh water in the lid every day.

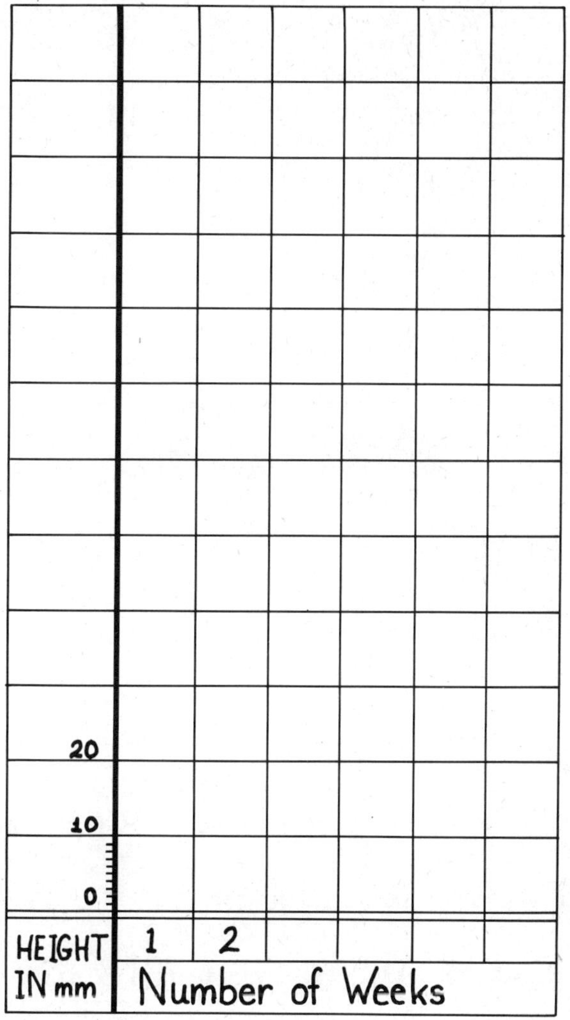

Measure the height of growth in mm every week.

Record the height on this grid. You will make a graph to show the growth.

Milli- and Car Widths

Patrick wants a car narrow enough to fit easily within parking lines for cars at your school and at shopping centers near your home. He found cars with these widths. Which widths should he consider?

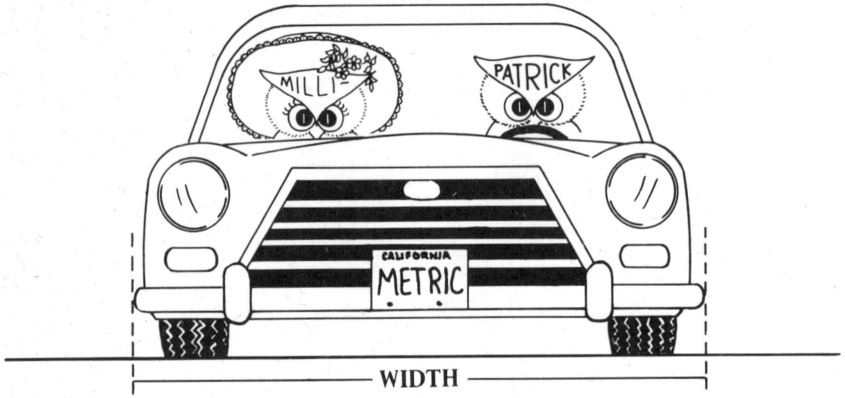

1644.75mm
1620.25mm
1615.25mm
1606.00mm
1587.5mm
1462.5mm
1450.0mm

Find the width in mm of a marked space for a car on a parking lot on your school ground or at a shopping center near your home. ______ mm

Circle the widths of the cars that would fit easily.

Cut strings as long as the above car widths. Order them on the wall.

How do the above widths compare with the width of your family car?

Measure widths of different kinds of cars. Include your family car, trucks, campers and a school bus. Record your data. Compare with these.

Car Lengths and Milli-

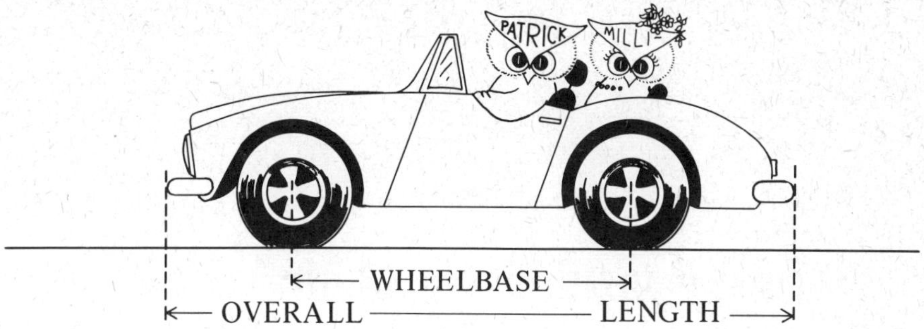

Patrick needs a car short enough to fit safely within lines marked for a parked car. He found cars with these dimensions, which are *actual* measurements:

	Wheelbase	Overall Length
Car A	2721.0 mm	4792.5 mm
Car B	2500.0 mm	4343.75 mm
Car C	2337.0 mm	4113 mm
Car D	2200.0 mm	3875 mm
Car E	2075.0 mm	3725 mm

Measure the length in mm of a space marked for a car. Will each car fit? *For each car that fits, find the difference between its overall length and the length of the parking marks. What is significant about wheelbase?

Hollywood Metrics

How many different widths of film can you find?________________

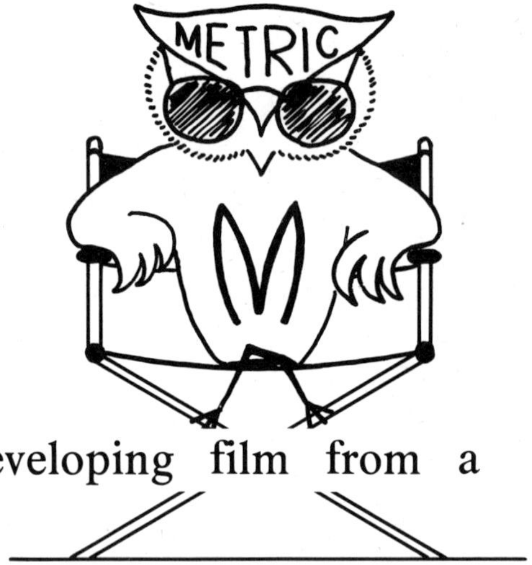

Draw lines to show these widths of film:

8 mm.

16 mm.

35 mm.

Get an order form with a price list for developing film from a photofinishing company.

How many times did you find "35 mm"?________________

How many times did you find "8 mm"? ________________

Investigate other sizes of film.

Kilometer

I know a Kilometer (Km) measures 1000 meters, but how long is 1000 meters?

If you don't know that, measure the distance of 100 meters. 100 meters is the length of a Hectometer. Measure the distance of 10 Hectometers (Hm) on your school yard. 10 Hectometers measure 1000 meters. That's a Kilometer.

Walk the kilometer. How long did it take?
*What was your time per meter? Your distance per min.?

Discovering Distances

Look at the road sign. What does it say? How many Km is that? To find out, we are going to learn how to use a Nomograph. Get a cm ruler.

Miles in 100's	Kilometers (Km)	Miles in tens	Kilometers (Km)	Miles in units	Kilometers (Km)
100	160	10	16	1	1.6
200	320	20	32	2	3.2
300	480	30	48	3	4.8
400	640	40	64	4	6.4
500	800	50	80	5	8
600	960	60	96	6	9.6
700	1120	70	112	7	11.2
800	1280	80	128	8	12.8
900	1440	90	144	9	14.4

Find the 5 under "Miles in units." Put your ruler straight across to find the equivalent in kilometers. Did you find 8 Km? Splendid! Change 60 miles to Km. Did you find 96 Km? Fine! Try some more! Find 125 miles. (8 + 32 + 160 =_____Km) Now find 748 miles =_____Km

*Look for road signs in miles. Use this Nomograph to change miles to Km.

Comparing Distances

inches	cm
1	2.5
2	5.0
3	7.5

The distance from Belmont to San Francisco is about 40.225 Km. We say the distance is about 40 Km.

From Belmont to San Mateo the distance is about 11.263 Km. Would you say the distance is about 11 Km, 11.3 Km or 12 Km? Why?

Belmont is on the peninsula between San Francisco Bay and the Pacific Ocean. It is a suburb in the Bay Area near San Francisco, California. In what area do you live?

Get a map of your area. Look for various distances on the map. Find these distances in Km. Use your nomograph.

*Make a line graph to show the distances in Km. Compare distances.

*Look at many different kinds of maps, especially road maps. Can you use different maps to compare the same distances? How? Look at the various scales. What unit usually stands for other units?

*Use the nomograph at the top of this page to find the equivalent in Metric units. Now look at maps with Metric scales. Compare some of the distances with distances in the region where you live.

Regulation Measurement

Estimate and check by measuring:

		Guess	Measure
BASEBALL:	base to base	________ m.	________ m.
	bat length	________ m.	________ m.
	home plate to pitcher's box	________ m.	________ m.
FOOTBALL:	height of goal posts	________ m.	________ m.
	length of field	________ m.	________ m.
	width of field	________ m.	________ m.
TENNIS:	length of court	________ m.	________ m.
	width of doubles' court	________ m.	________ m.
	width of singles' court	________ m.	________ m.
	service line to net	________ m.	________ m.
	height of tennis net	________ m.	________ m.
BASKETBALL:	length of playing court	________ m.	________ m.
	width of playing court	________ m.	________ m.
	inside diameter of the basket	________ m.	________ m.
	height of basket ring from the floor	________ m.	________ m.

Metric Measurements

Use the distance between your index fingers or draw a line to show these lengths:

1 millimeter (mm) 1 decimeter (dm)

1 centimeter (cm) 1 meter or 1 m

Write measurements in appropriate Metric units to show these distances:

from school to your home ____ the length of your family car ____

the length of your index finger ____ length of a car key ____

length of one edge of a stere ____ diameter of a half dollar ____

total length of all edges of a stere ____ width of this page ____

*If a length of 1 meter 2 decimeters 9 centimeters is removed from a length of 4 meters 7 centimeters, how many meters are left?______m

*"Make a Meter" game is appropriate here. See Appendix.

AREA

Hand Graphs

Place your hand on cm grid paper. Be sure your fingers are touching. Trace around your hand.

How much paper is covered? Count the cm squares. ______ cm^2

How much paper is covered if you spread your fingers apart?

Now try your left foot.

How many hands does it take to cover as much paper as your foot?

Do you think this is about the same for all people?

See if you can decide. How could you find the data you need?

*Measure the surface other things will cover. Use cm grid paper. Count the covered squares. (The area of each square is 1 cm^2. What do you think you should do about partially-covered squares? Why?)

Animal Graphs

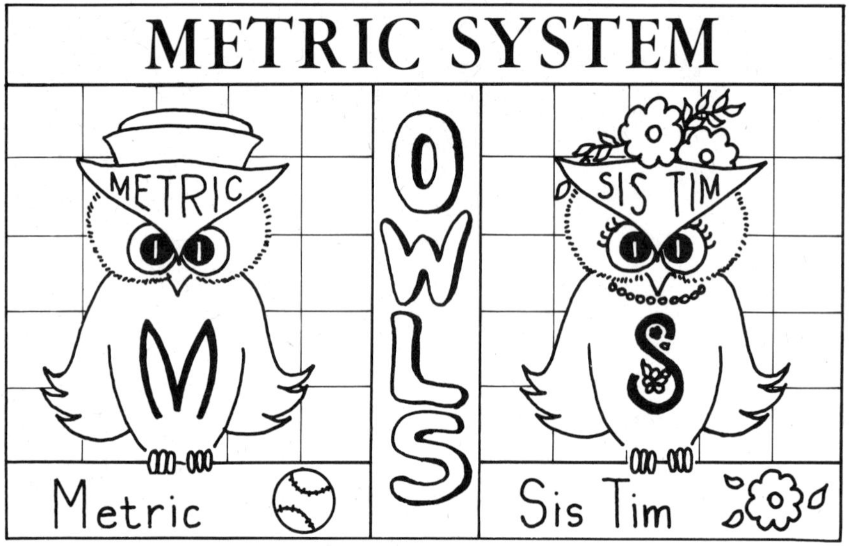

Color Metric.

How many squares did you color? ____ cm^2

Color Sis Tim.

How many squares did you color? ______ cm^2

How many squares did both owls cover? _______ cm^2

Draw some other animals on cm grid paper. Color them if you wish.

Which drawing is the biggest?

Which is the smallest?

How many squares does each animal cover?

How can you tell for sure?

Comparing Leaves

Collect six different leaves. Outline them on cm grid paper. Count the squares covered by each leaf.

What was the greatest number of squares covered by a leaf?

What was the smallest number of squares covered by a leaf?

By counting the squares under each leaf can you find the relative sizes of your leaves? Try it.

Order the sizes of your leaves from the smallest to the largest.

*How would you find the area of each leaf? Find the total area.

Grid Blob

You will need a cm grid that is transparent.

You will use the grid to find the area of this shape.

Put your transparent grid on top of this shape.

Count the squares. _____ cm^2

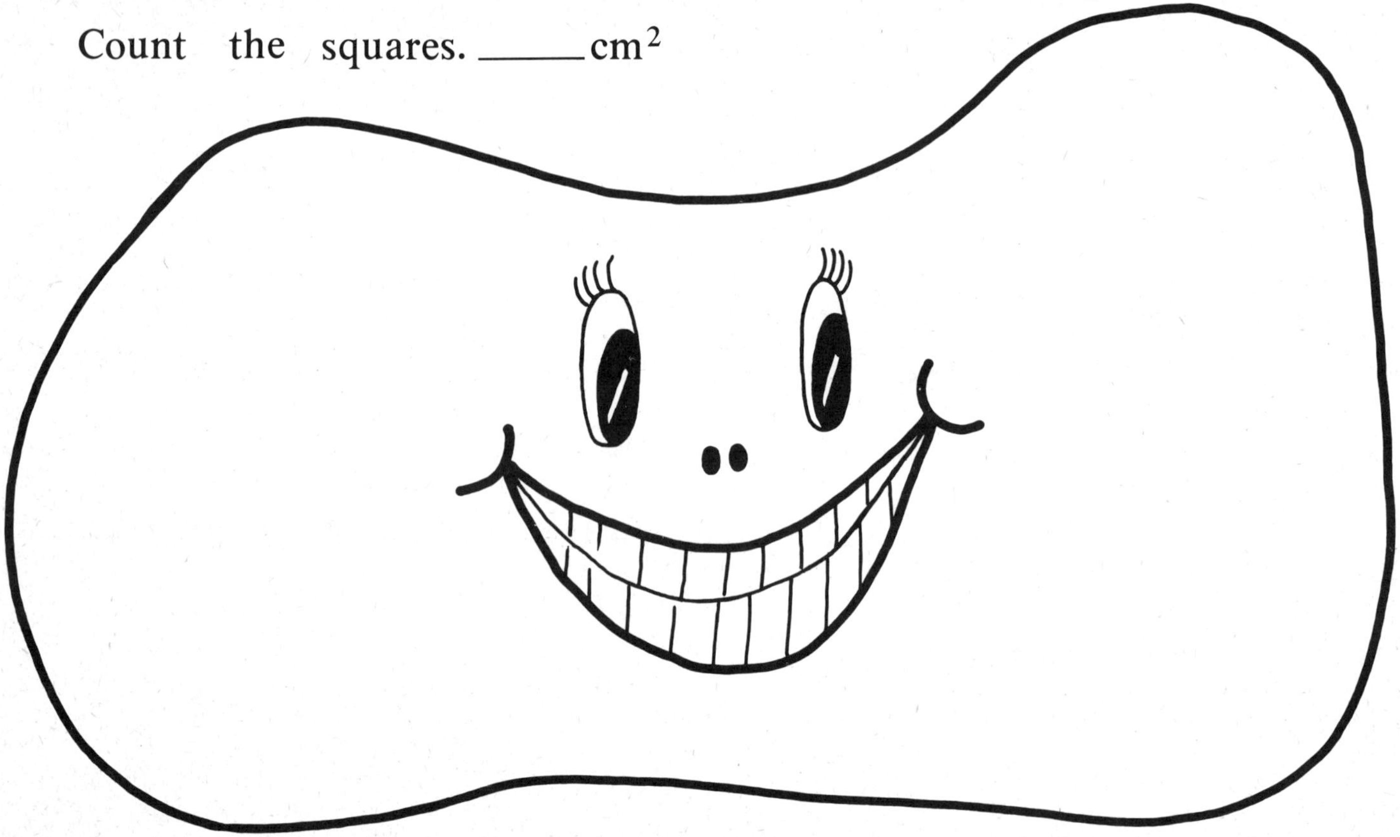

Draw your own shapes and find the area in cm^2.

Wise Owls "Metric-ize"

A wise pupil can metric-ize with sharp eyes!

He can see an approximate size, if he tries.

Do you see this square? Can you guess its size?

Each side of the square is ______ cm.

The area is ______ cm^2.

Measure to check your estimation. Cut out the square.

Use it to find out how many you need to cover the surface of Metric's picture. About ______ cm^2.

The number of squares you need is the area in cm^2.

Use the square to find how many will cover other pictures.

What's Area?

Patrick wants to know.

He *needs* your help.

Patrick knows that the length of his rectangle is_____cm and the width is_____cm. He wants to find the area of his rectangle. Let's help Patrick.

First, look at the square on top of his head.

Each side of the square measures_____cm. The area of the square is one square centimeter.

Cut out the square. Use it to find how many square centimeters will cover the inside of his rectangle_____ sq. cm.

What's Area?(Contd.)

How many square centimeters will cover the inside of Patrick's rectangle?______square cm.

Ten square centimeters is the area of his rectangle.

Use your centimeter square to find the area of these rectangles:

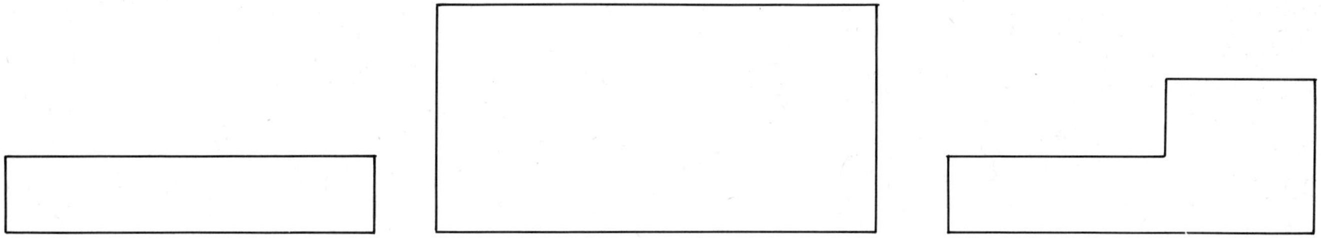

Area =___square cm   Area =___sq. cm   Area =___sq. cm

Find the area of this page. The area is______sq. cm.

Use your centimeter square to find the area of other rectangles in this room.

Area of A Catch

Use a transparent cm grid to find the area of the catch on this line!

The area of the catch was _____ cm^2.

Use the grid to find other areas: Metric with all his fishing gear _____ cm^2

the bottom of your shoe _____ cm^2 top of an oatmeal box _____ cm^2

Put your grid over other flat surfaces and find the area in cm^2.

Record your areas on this sign.

*Why did we count the squares to find each area in square centimeters?

Label Maker

Select a tin can with no label.

Cut out a rectangular piece of paper that fits around the curved surface of the can. It should be an exact fit, like a label without overlap.

Now find the area of the curved surface of the can. _____ cm^2

Check your work. Find the area a different way by counting cm squares:

Cut out enough cm squares to cover the paper or the can.

Use a ruler and draw cm squares on the rectangular piece of paper.

Cut out and use only 1 cm square. Use cm grid paper or transparency.

Can you think of another way to find the area? Try out your own ideas.

Design a label for your favorite canned food. Design one for the owls.

Square Decimeter

You will need some decimeter squares (dm^2). You will have to make them.

Find a flat place and cover it with dm squares.

Find the area by counting the dm squares.

____dm^2

To check your work, have your partner find the area a different way.

Compare your answers.

Can you find the area of the sink counter in your classroom?

Can you find the area by using only *one* of your decimeter squares?____dm^2

*Find the areas of other flat surfaces on furniture. Do it a quick way.

Chalkboard Chance

Estimate the area of the chalkboard in square meters (m^2).

Write your estimate._____ m^2

Measure the chalkboard dimensions, and find the area._____ m^2

Compare the two areas in m^2.

Did you make a reasonable estimate? Compare your work with that of a classmate.

What is a reasonable result?

*Find the area of the classroom floor._____ m^2 Find other areas.

*Estimate the cost of carpeting the floor. Compute actual cost at $19/$m^2$.

Square Your Meter

Use a meter stick and make a line 1 meter long on some butcher paper.

Put your math book at the corner like this: 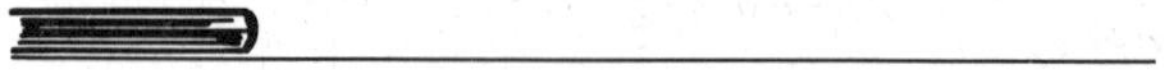

Use the book to help you make a square corner.

Draw another line 1 meter long. Did you make a square corner?

What do we call a square corner?

Now make two more lines 1 meter long to make a square meter. Cut out your square meter. Is it big? As big as what? Invite one or two friends to help you cover your square meter with square decimeters. Select gay colored paper to make your dm squares. Paste them on the m^2.

How many decimeter squares did you need?____dm^2 That's the area of your square meter in square decimeters. Make a jig-saw puzzle out of the M^2.

Shades of Windows

How many square meters of shade material would you need to make new window shades for your classroom? ____m^2. How much would the shade material cost for each window?

How much would shade material for all the windows cost?

Show your calculations on the back of this worksheet.

*How many square meters of shade material is required to make new window shades for every window in your school? Show your calculations.

Square Games

What are the dimensions of a four-square? ________

What is the area? ________

What are the dimensions of each square in a four square? ________

What is the area of each small square in a four-square? ________

What are the dimensions of a checkerboard, regulation size? ________

Find the area. ____ mm^2 ____ cm^2 ____ dm^2 ____ m^2

What are the dimensions of a chess board, regulation size? ________

Find the area.

Play a game of chess, checkers or four-square.

*Find costs of chess boards per cm^2.

*Make a graph to show your data.

*"SURFACE" game would be appropriate here. See Appendix.

Four-Square

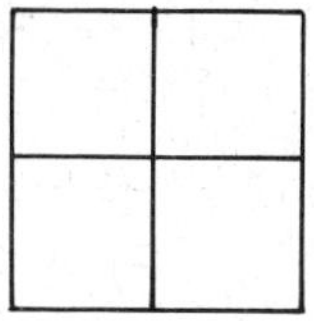

Find these distances:

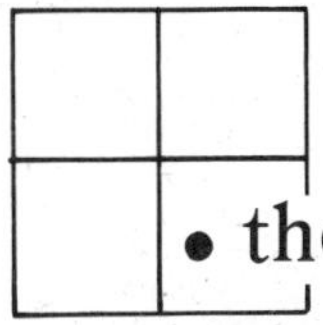

- the length in meters of each side of a four-square painted on the playground and used for games _____ m
- the length in meters of the four sides (perimeter) _____ m
- the perimeter of one of the four small squares ____ m

Do you think a decimeter would be a better unit for measuring the sides of a small square that is part of a four-square? If so, try it.

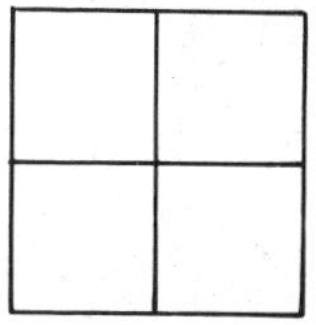

Can you find the area of the four-square? ____ m^2

*Can you find the area of the four-square another way?

*If you wanted to paint a new line on all 16 sides of the 4 small squares and on the 4 sides of the big square, what is the total length of line you would have to paint on the old lines of the four-square?

Squares

How many square centimeters are needed to cover each of these?

this page _______ top of a penny _______

the curved surface of a buffet-size can _______

the surface on the sole of your left shoe _______

Under each of the above phrases write the area in cm^2.

How many square decimeters are needed to cover each of these?

this page _______ the top of your desk _______

Under each of the above phrases write the area in dm^2.

What is a reasonable estimate for the area of the floor of the classroom in square meters?

*How many square meters will cover a square kilometer? _______

*What is the area in millimeters (mm) of the top surface of a half dollar? ________ mm^2 of a rectangle 10 cm x 10 dm? _____

A Little Square □

Name 5 surfaces most appropriately measured with each of these units:

square centimeters　　square decimeters
square kilometers　　square meters
square millimeters

State estimates of areas in square units of the metric system:

a paper towel ________ curved surface of a soup can ________
a circular region with a diameter of 1 dm ________
a four-square marked on a playground for four-square games ________
surface of the chalkboard ________ the top of a straight pin ________
the top of a bookcase in the classroom ________

*After removing $3dm^2$, $10cm^2$ and $100mm^2$ from $5m^2$, what remains? ______

Turning Circles

Patrick wanted a car with a small turning area. He expected measurements of diameters in meters but when he checked the data supplied by dealers, he found mm units for diameters of turning circles.

	cm	dm	m	Area
10,000 mm				
9753 mm				
7700 mm				
6200 mm				

Change the mm to cm, dm and m. (1000 mm = 100 cm = 10 dm = 1 m)

On the schoolyard measure circles with diameters in mm as given.

Compute the area of each turning circle. Record the area in mm^2.

*Compute the area in mm^2 of the turning area for your family car.

Record the area in mm^2. ________ mm^2 Get more data from dealers.

Make a Muu-muu

Get an old shirt. Cut off the sleeves any length, or cut them out entirely. You will decorate the front of your shirt-made-over.

Draw or trace a big picture of Metric, Sis Tim or Patrick Owl.

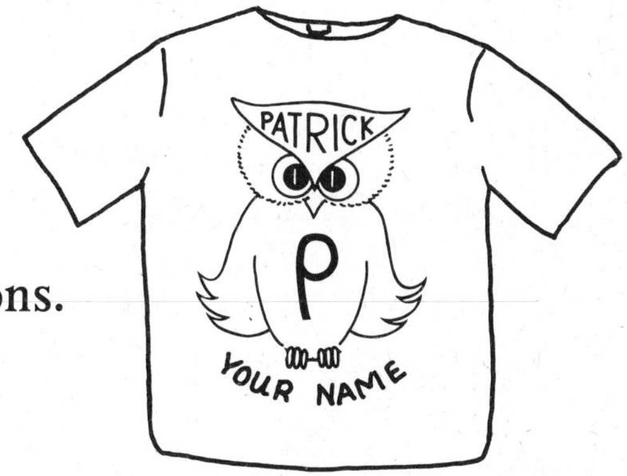

Color heavily with bright colored wax crayons.

Color your own name and cut off the collar. Put the completed picture between two 30 cm squares of wax paper. Use a hot iron to press the colors into the cloth, or let someone do it for you. Now you have made a muu-muu that really isn't a muu-muu at all but a Cooking Apron or a Painting Protector. Use it in school.

CAPACITY or VOLUME

Metric Table for Capacity

A liter is the Standard Unit

One liter = 1.057 qts.

One qt. = .9461 liter

1 myrialiter = 10,000 liters

1 kiloliter = 1,000 liters

1 hectoliter = 100 liters

1 decaliter = 10 liters

1 liter = 1 liter

1 deciliter = .1 liter

1 centiliter = .01 liter

1 milliliter = .001 liter

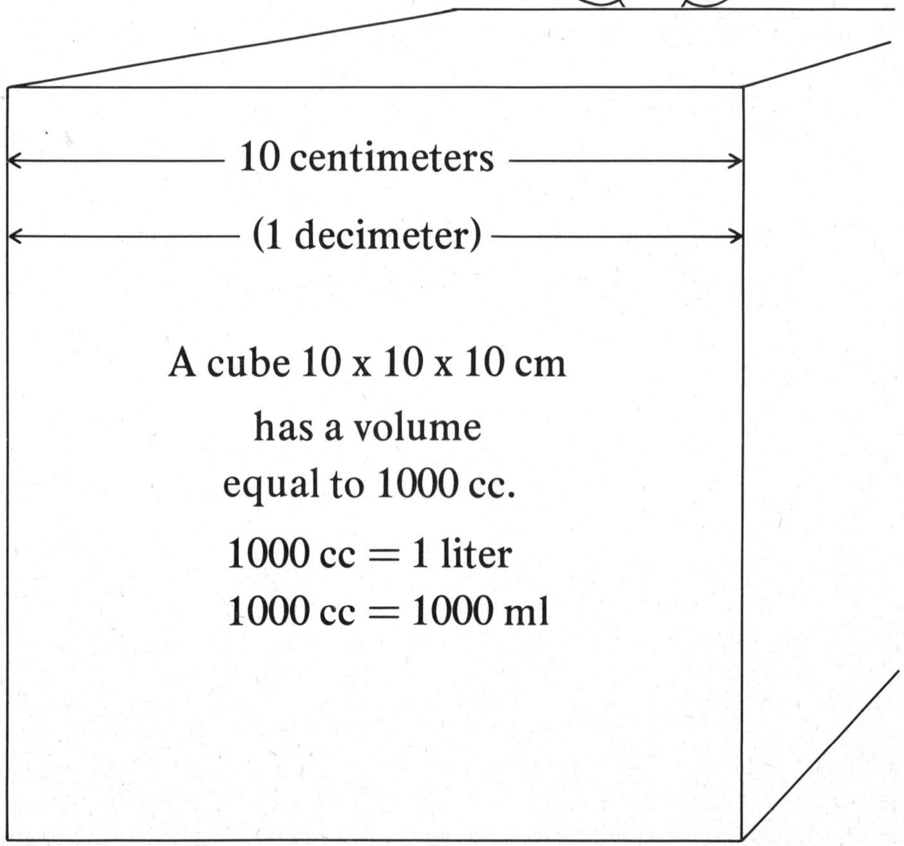

Decimeter Cube

Make a cube with a measurement of 10 cm on each edge. That's ____ dm.

Use construction paper measuring 22.5 by 30 cm.

Figure out how to make the cube yourself.

How many edges are in your cube? 12

What is the measurement of each edge in dm? 1 dm and in cm? 10

The flat surfaces of a cube are called faces.

How many faces does your cube have?

What is the area of each face in cm^2? ____ cm^2 And in ____ dm^2

Cut away one face of your cube to make a square box without a top.

Fill the box with centimeter cubes. Count the cubes. ______ cm^3

That is the volume of your decimeter cube.

You should have counted 1000 centimeter cubes. Did you?

If you didn't count 1000 cm cubes, something is wrong. Try again!

Spare Time X

Make a decimeter cube. Use colored construction paper 22.5 cm x 30 cm.

How many faces does your cube have? How many edges?

How long is each edge? _____ dm or _____ cm or _____ mm

How many decimeter cubes would you have to put in a line to measure the length of a meter?

Make a line of decimeter cubes one meter long.

You may want to work with others to do this.

You may also want to borrow cubes from other pupils.

Measure the line of ten decimeter cubes. Do they measure about a meter? How could you find the volume of a cubic meter?

How many decimeter cubes would you need to show the volume of a cubic meter?

We shall try to make enough decimeter cubes to measure the volume of a meter. Begin now. During your spare time you may continue.

Stere: A Cubic Meter

We are going to show the dimensions of a cubic meter, which is sometimes called a stere.

You will need narrow sticks like molding.

You will need as many sticks as there are edges on a cube.

Work with one or two friends so you can make square corners.

How many people do you think would fit inside your frame?

Measure the number of people who fit by counting the people inside your frame. Their heads may be no higher than a meter.

How many people did you count? ________

For what could you use your frame?

Plan something useful or plan something for fun. Try your ideas.

*What is the capacity of the stere? ______ What is the volume? ______

For what purposes do you think a stere is used?

Boxes of Cubes

Make a centimeter cube out of cm squares cut from a cm grid.

Cut away one face.

What is the capacity of your cm box?

How can you find out what the capacity is?

Do you know what the volume of your centimeter cube was?____ cm^3

Fill your cm box with sand. Pour the sand into a ml graduate.

Measure the quantity of sand._____ ml

Measure a box full of other things in a ml graduate.

Get some plastic or wooden centimeter cubes.

Get many small boxes of different shapes and sizes but with square corners.

Fill each box with centimeter cubes.

To find the volume of each box, count the cubes.

Decipede

A Make-believe Creature

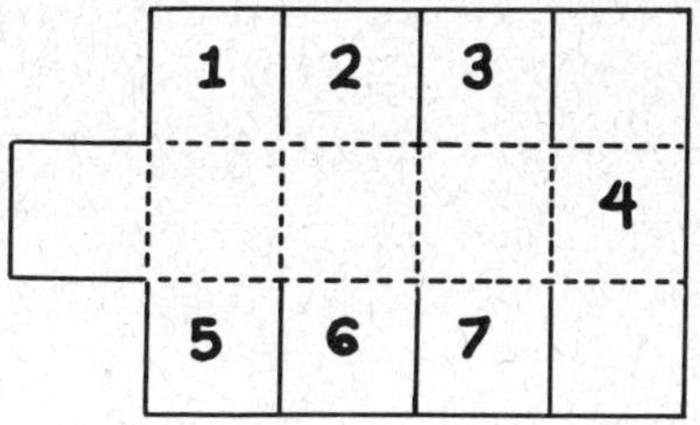

Measure the square on your left. What is the area?______cm^2

Yes, the area is one cm^2. Cut out the centimeter square. Use the square to find out how many will cover the upper-right figure.

What is the area of the figure?______cm^2

Cut out the upper-right figure. Now cut along the unbroken lines. Fold the broken lines to make the edges of a cube.

To make a cube, put glue on the numbered squares. Make the cube. Each square surface is called a face. Count the faces.______cm^2

Cut a string 60 mm long. Cut it into five 12 mm pieces.

To make ten legs, each 1 mm long, glue the string on one face like this: 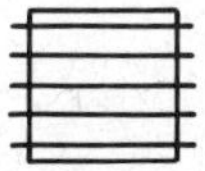

Make a face for your Decipede.

Save your Decipede, a Make-believe Creature.

*Make more cm cubes without patterns.

Decimeter Centipede

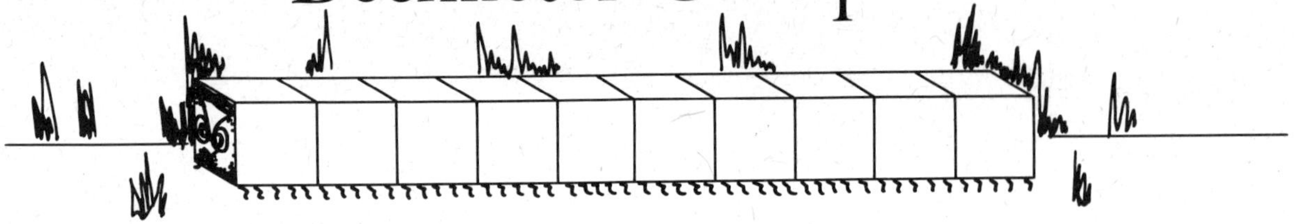

Make ten 1 centimeter cubes.

Cut a string 60 mm long. Cut it into five 12 mm pieces.

Glue the 5 pieces of string on one face of a cube.

You will have 5 legs on each side. Try to make each leg 1 mm long.

Cut string and make 10 legs for each cube.

Put a funny face on the square surface of one cube.

The cube with the funny face will be the head of your make-believe creature.

Put the 9 other cubes in a row behind the first one.

Glue all the cubes together in a row.

You have made a Decimeter Centipede, a Make-believe Creature.

How do you think the Decimeter Centipede got its name?

How do you think the Decipede got its name?

Measure the length of your Decimeter Centipede.____cm or _____dm

Put ten Decimeter Centipedes in a row and measure them. ________

Meter Millipede

Work with ten friends who have made Decimeter Centipedes.

Put the Centipedes end to end in one row and glue them together.

Now you have made Meter Millipede.

How long is Meter Millipede?

____ mm or ____ cm or ____ dm or ____ m

How many legs does Meter Millipede have?

If each leg is 1 mm long, what is the total length of her legs?

____ mm or ____ cm or ____ dm or ____ m

If the capacity of each centimeter cube is 1 milliliter (ml), what is the total capacity of Meter Millipede?_____ ml or_____ 1

What is her volume in centimeter cubes?_____ cm^3 or_____ cc

cc is one way to write cubic centimeter. Another way is ____.

A cubic centimeter (cc or cm^3) is equivalent to _____ ml.

*How many Meter Millipedes would you need to fill a Stere (m^3)?____

Legs Count Legs

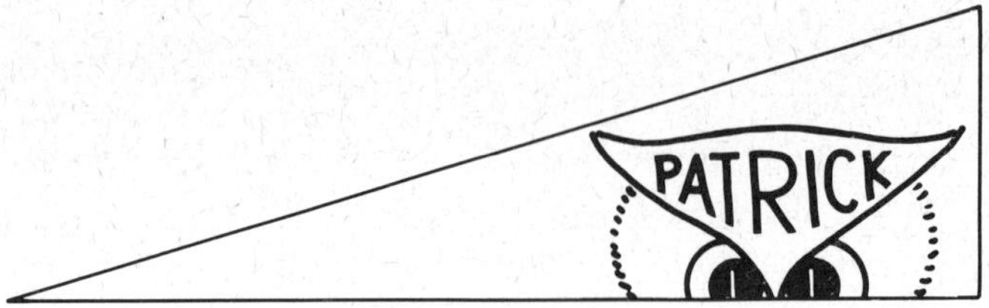

Get out your Make-believe Creatures.

Decipede is the centimeter cube. How many legs does it have?

How many legs does Decimeter Centipede have?

If each of Decipede's legs is 1 mm long, how long are all 10?____mm

10 mm is equivalent to ____cm. That's the length of Decipede.

What should be the total length of Decimeter Centipede's legs?____mm

100 mm is equivalent to ____cm or ____dm

How long is Decimeter Centipede?____mm or ____cm or ____dm

Put ten Decimeter Centipedes end to end in one line.

How long are all ten?____mm or____cm or ____dm or ____meter

How many legs do all ten Decimeter Centipedes have?______

What is the total length of all the legs on all ten?______

10^2

The total length of their legs is:______mm

1000 mm is equivalent to____cm or____dm or____m

We could find out all these things by counting legs of the creatures.

Exploring Capacities

Use your graduate calibrated in milliliters (ml).

Measure the capacities in ml of plastic containers of many sizes.

Order the plastic containers according to their capacities in ml.

Put the container with the smallest capacity first.

Put the container with the largest capacity last.

Put the other containers in the right order.

Use your graduate to measure the capacity of these containers:

a teaspoon______ml a tablespoon_____ml a cup______

Find the capacity of other containers which interest you.

Record the capacities in ml on the back of this page.

Measure the capacity of a liter container._____ml

Use the liter container to measure the number of liters in pots and pans.

Measure the number of liters in a bucket.____1 Measure other capacities.

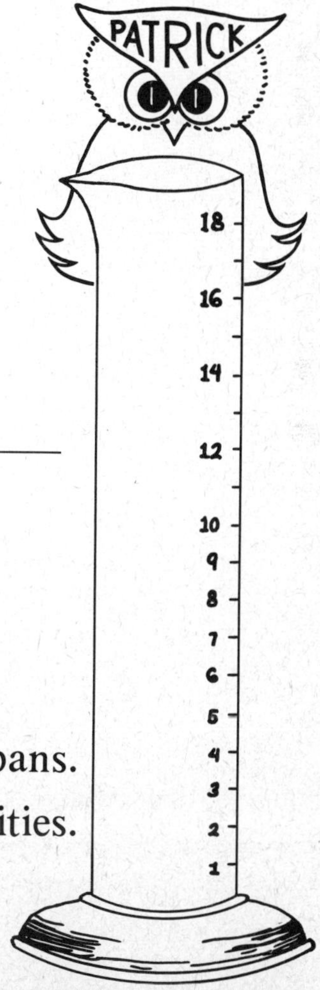

Decorating

Find out how many liters of paint it would take to paint all the walls in your classroom. ____ liters

How much would the paint cost?

NOTE: 3.785 liters of semi gloss enamel covers approximately 51.5 square meters so 1 liter covers approximately 132.2m^2. Use 133 m^2: 1 liter covers 133 square meters.

Find out how much wall paper it would take to cover all the walls in your classroom. ________ How much would the wallpaper cost? ________

NOTE: Contractors subtract the area of the doors and windows from total wall area which is calculated by using room height and floor perimeter as dimensions. Wall paper is sold by the roll, usually containing 548.64 cm of various widths of paper. The most common width is 60.96 cm.

*Which would be cheaper: wall papering or painting your classroom? Remember to include the cost of labor.

A Room Full

Find the distance around a basketball.

Estimate how many basketballs it would take to fill your classroom.

How much would this many balls cost?

Find the distance around a tennis ball.
Estimate how many tennis balls it would take to fill your classroom.
How much would these tennis balls cost?
Compare prices. Which costs more?
*Estimate the number of steres it would take to fill the classroom.
Estimate the number of kiloliters of water at 4°C and at 760mm pressure it would take to fill your classroom. How many Metric tons of water?

A Graduate

Make or find a box the same size as a decimeter cube.

Check to be sure that your box is the right size.

Fill your box with cm cubes. Count the cubes. ______ cm^3

If you counted 1000 cm^3 you may continue. If not, find your error.

The volume of your box should be 1000 cubic centimeters (cm^3).

Fill up your box with rice.

Get a graduate marked in milliliters (ml). This is a graduate.

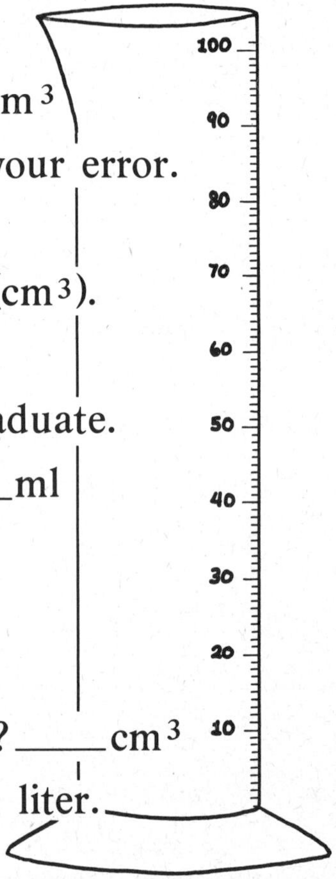

Use the graduate to measure the rice in your box. ______ ml

Did you measure 1000 ml? If not, try again.

1000 ml is equivalent to a liter. But what is a liter?

You measured the rice that filled a box of what volume? ______ cm^3

So 1000 cubic centimeters is equivalent to ______ ml or 1 liter.

The capacity of your box was 1 liter or ______ ml.

Cans Cans Cans

Use metric balances or scales to weigh the following sizes of cans filled with food.

Size of Can	Weight with Food	Capacity of Empty Can
Buffet	__________	__________
#1	__________	__________
#303	__________	__________
#2	__________	__________
#2½	__________	__________
#3	__________	__________
#10	__________	__________
Others	__________	__________

Use a ml graduate to find the capacity of each can.

*Find the volume of each of these:

Whole egg	8 to 9 whites of eggs
Five whole eggs	12 yolks of eggs

Fuel Tanks

The fuel tank in Patrick's old car has a capacity of 94.525 liters (approximately 94.5 liters or 25 gallons). Fuel tank capacities of new cars he is considering buying include these:

90.84 liters	44.2845 liters
61.7525 liters	43.1498 liters
53.785 liters	41.625 liters
49.205 liters	32.9295 liters
45.42 liters	30.0085 liters

Write the above equivalents in gallons.

Patrick was returning home from the pet store with two *litters* of kittens in the car when he stopped for 90 *liters* of gasoline. He let the kittens play with charcoal *lighters.*

How do you pronounce "liters" of gas? (the *i* in liter has the long *e* sound as in Lee or in Meet.) Incidentally, did you remember to use a nomograph to find the number of gallons?

*"MEET'ER LITER" game is appropriate here. See Appendix.

Estimating Capacity

(a review of capacity)

Put < , > or = between each set.

1 liter _____ 1 quart

1000 milliliters _____ 1 quart

1000 ml _____ 1 liter

1 liter _____ 1 gallon

10 liters _____ 1 gallon

1 liter _____ tablespoon

Give the approximate capacities in metric units (appropriate ones) of the following:

#2 can _____

gas tank on a car _______

a cup _______

Measure to check your answers.

Metric Molds

Measure 120 ml mashed potato (You may use instant potatoes.)

5 ml almond flavoring

30 ml margarine

Combine the above and add: 480 ml powdered sugar, sifted

Combine the above and add: 240 ml powdered milk

Chill. Knead in enough sugar to handle well. Shape into tiny fruits and vegetables. Paint with food coloring.

You can eat these.

MASS (WEIGHT)

Metric Table for Mass

1 myriagram = 10,000 grams
1 kilogram = 1,000 grams
1 hectogram = 100 grams
1 decagram = 10 grams
1 gram = gram
1 decigram = .1 gram
1 centigram = .01 gram
1 milligram = .001 gram

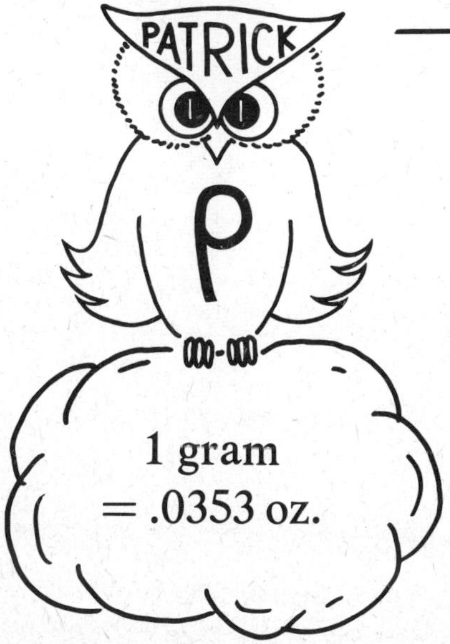

A gram is the Standard Unit

Gram Equivalents

.0001 myriagram
.001 kilogram
.01 hectogram
.1 decagram
1 gram
10 decigrams = 1 gram
100 centigrams = 1 gram
1000 milligrams = 1 gram

"Metric-ize" Balance

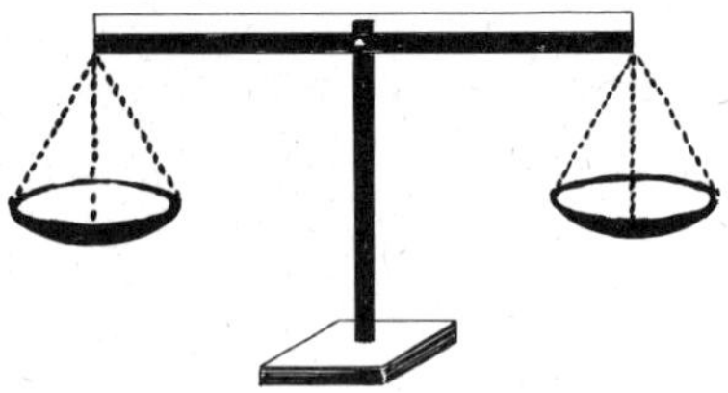

Which do you think is the heaviest?

a liter of peas? a liter of beans? a liter of oatmeal?

Write your estimate, then use the balance to check your estimate.

Which is heavier, a liter of beans or a liter of rice?

Estimate first then measure.

Find other things to compare. Always estimate then measure.

Can you make reasonable estimates?

*How could you find the weight in grams of 1 cubic cm of sand without Metric weights?

A Good Balance

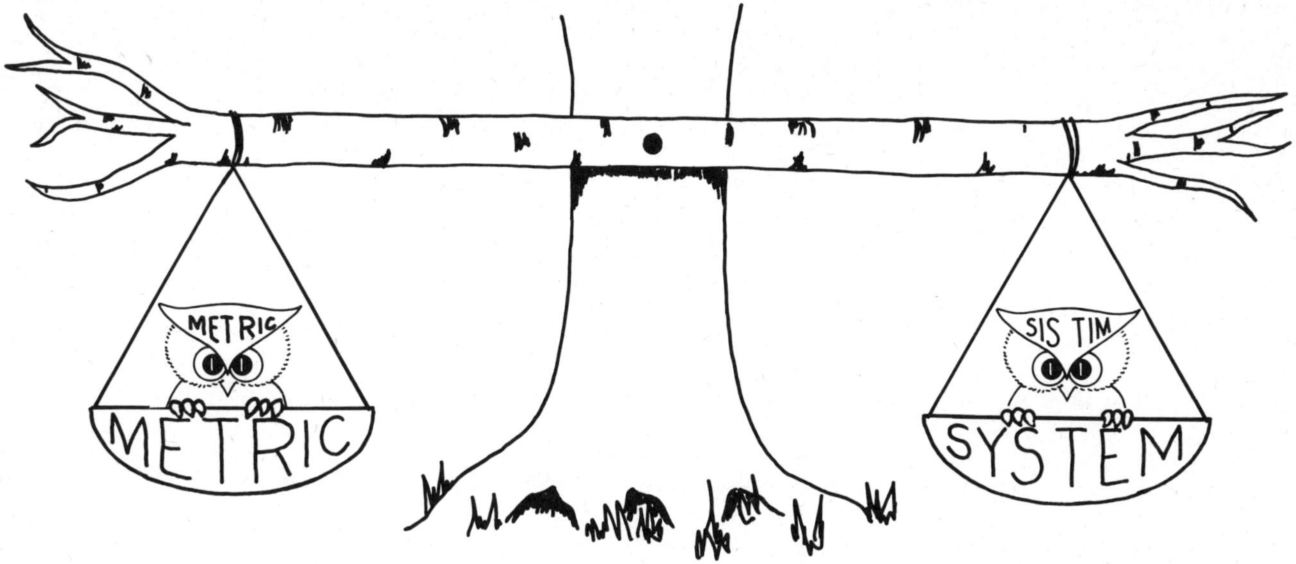

Compare the amount of rice needed to balance a liter of flour. Use a graduate to measure the amount of rice you needed. Record data. Compare the amount of rice needed to balance each of the following:

football full of air	a rubber band	a cork
deflated football	chip of wood	apple

Which substance required the largest amount of rice for a balance?

Balance a Liter

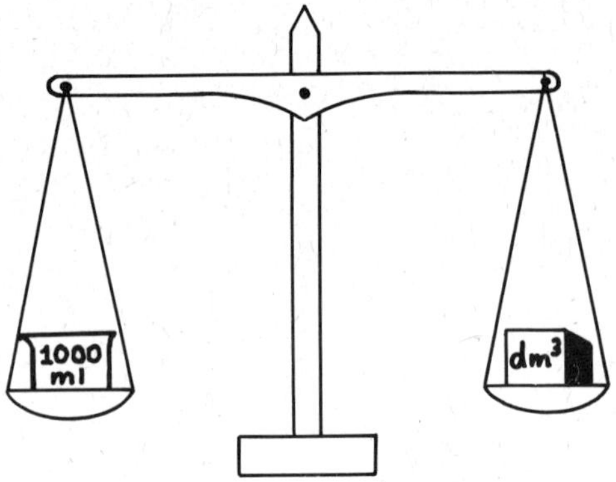

You will need two plastic containers of the same size and large enough to hold a liter of matter. Use plastic beakers if you have them. Use a graduate to measure a liter of water. Pour the water into a beaker. Put it on one side of the balance. You will compare the liter of water with a liter of each of the following:

whole milk	sand	detergent	molasses
pebbles	nails	marbles	shredded styrofoam

Did a liter of each of these balance a liter of water?

Not Litter or Lighter! A Liter!

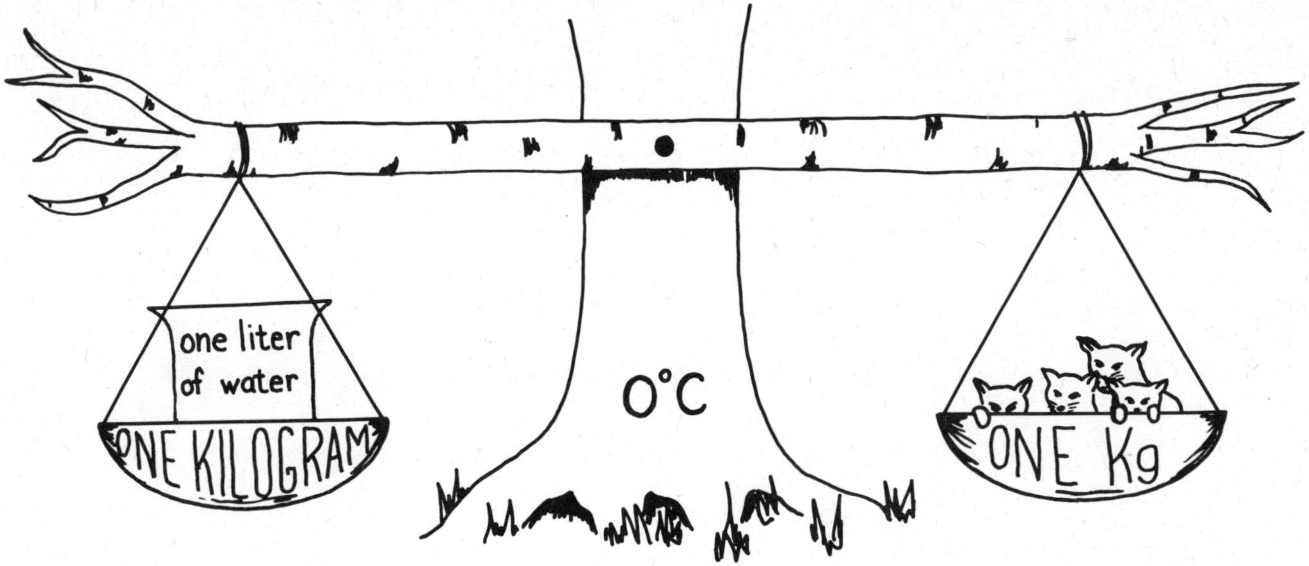

Get a set of Metric weights and examine each weight.

See how many different ways you can arrange the weights so they balance.

Use the weights to balance other objects in the classroom.

What conclusions can you make?

What Do You Weigh?

What do you weigh
in kilograms?

________kg

How many grams is that?

________g

Weigh three classmates and record
their weights in kilograms.

1. ________ kilograms
2. ________ kg.
3. ________ kg

*"SLAM-GRAM" game is appropriate here. See Appendix.

Dime-a-Gram

Weigh as many objects as you can find that weigh less than 450 grams. Record your findings on the back of this page.
Estimate the weight of these objects. Record your estimates.
Then weigh each one.

a hen's egg	a dime	a cubic centimeter of water
a liter of water	a cube of butter	a paper clip
a music book	a road map	an apple

Underline your most reasonable estimates.
Which object could you use for comparing weights?
Use it to estimate the weights of a tablespoon of salt and three teaspoons of salt. Use metric weights to check your estimates. Record your present weight in kilograms and in grams. Why does this page have the title Dime-a-Gram?

Regulation Balls

Weigh each regulation ball and record the weight of each in kilograms.

Baseball
Basketball
Bowling Ball
Football
Golf Ball
Other Balls

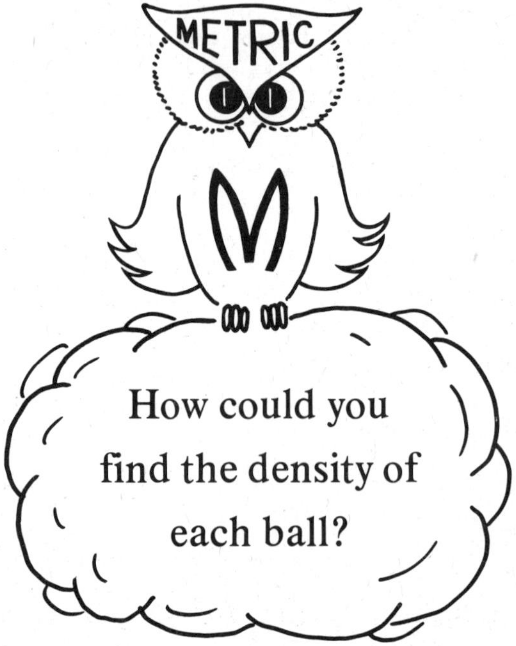

Convert the kg of each ball to other Metric Units. Include Mg, Hg, Dg, dg, cg and mg.

Fudge Gone Metric

You will use these ingredients:

80 g cream cheese (at room temperature)

454 g Powdered sugar

106.5 g unsweetened chocolate-flavored product
(comes in liquid form in envelopes)

2.5 ml Vanilla

320 ml Chopped nuts

25 g Butter

How to make the fudge:

1. Put cream cheese into the bowl.
2. Add half the powdered sugar, a little at a time. Stir and add.
3. Add the chocolate-flavored product.
4. Add the rest of the powdered sugar, a little at a time.
5. Stir in nuts and vanilla.
6. Butter the pan.
7. Put the fudge in the pan. Spread it evenly.
8. Chill the fudge for two hours or longer.
9. Wash bowl, spoon and other tools you used.
10. When the fudge is firm, cut it into squares, 3 cm^2 per square.

Metric Mints

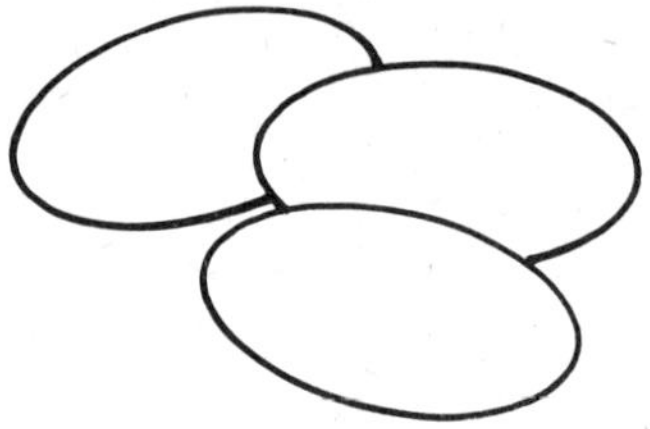

227 g cream cheese
114 g powdered sugar
10 ml mint or wintergreen flavoring
2 or 3 ml green food coloring

Put all ingredients into a mixing bowl. Mix well and set aside.

Cut a piece of wax paper about 30 cm x 30 cm.

Put a small pile of left-over sugar on the paper.

Dip your clean fingers in the pile of sugar.

Take a teaspoon of your mixture out of the mixing bowl.

Take the mixture out of the teaspoon and roll it in the sugar.

Roll it into a marble-sized ball. Flatten the ball into a 2 or 3 cm mint.

This recipe will make 25 mints.

Evaluate Your Progress

Place $>$ or $<$ between each pair.

apple	lg
car	10 km
one yard	1m
doorway	10 mm
most men	175 kg
one mile	1 km
pencil	1m
one quart	1 liter
one gallon	1 liter
school bus	10 cm
one cup	20 ml

Measure to check your estimates.

TEMPERATURE

NOMOGRAPH FOR TEMPERATURE CONVERSIONS

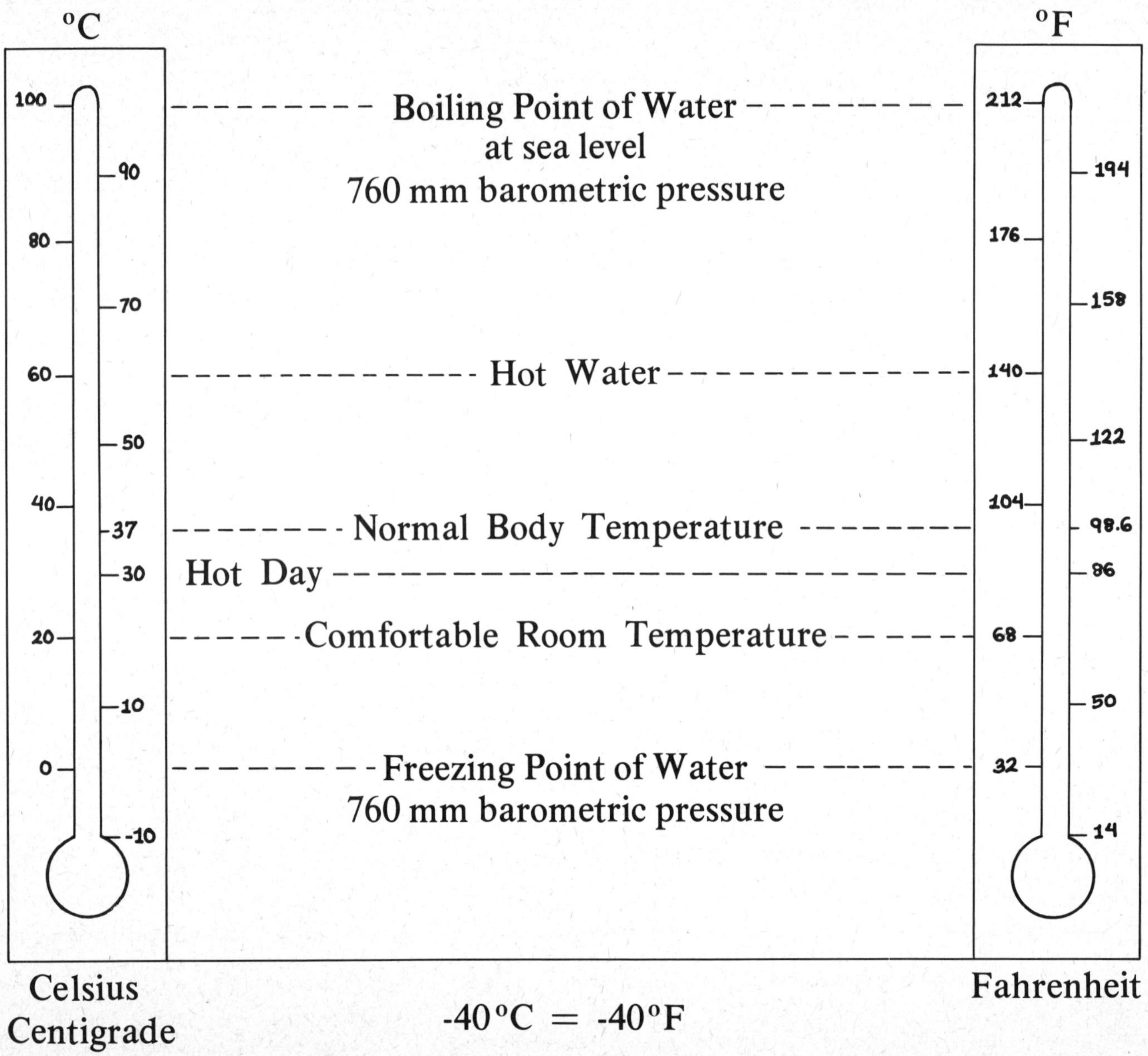

Thumbs and Thermometers

Does the thumb make the difference?
What happens when you leave your thumb over the bulb at the bottom of a thermometer for a while?
What happens when you take your thumb away?
What happens when you put your thumb at the top of the thermometer?
Report your findings.

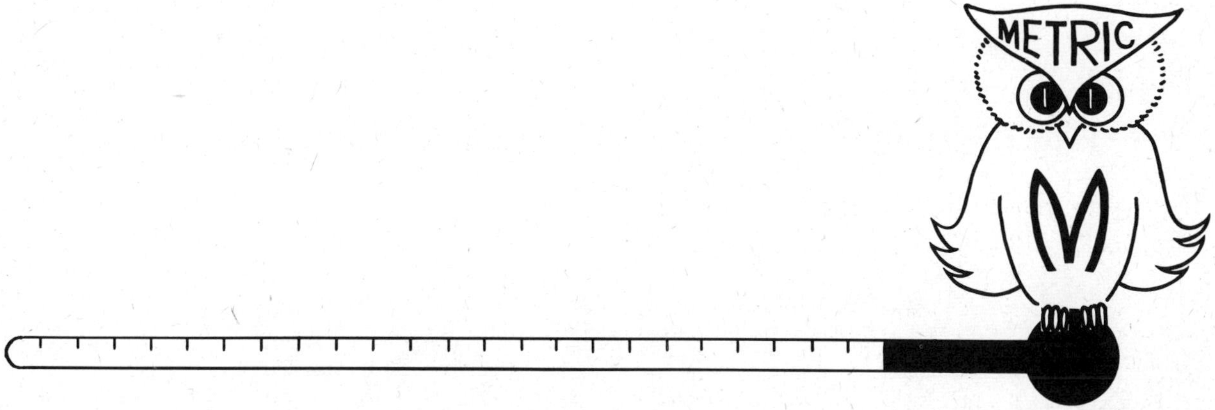

*Take the temperature in centigrade degrees of water containing ice cubes._______°C. Temperature of boiling water _______°C.

Sun and Shade

Is the temperature the same in the sun as in the shade? Place one thermometer in the shade and one in the sun. Each hour record the temperatures measured in centigrade degrees on both thermometers. Make a line graph.

Show the shade temperature in blue and the sun temperature in red. Report your findings.

Weather Reports

Look in newspapers for weather reports.

Every day for five days record temperatures in degrees centigrade (C). If temperatures in the weather reports are given in degrees Fahrenheit (F), use a temperature nomograph to find degrees centigrade. (C)

Record the lowest and highest temperatures given in each report.

Record the temperature reported for the location most distant from your home. Record the temperature where your school is located.

Use a Celsius-centigrade thermometer to find the temperatures in your classroom and outside in the shade. Record both temperatures in degrees C. Compare temperatures.

*Make graphs to show temperature differences.

For instance, use blue for the temperatures you took outside your classroom and red for the temperatures reported in newspapers.

*Compare the accuracy of temperature forecasts with actual temperatures.

Weatherman

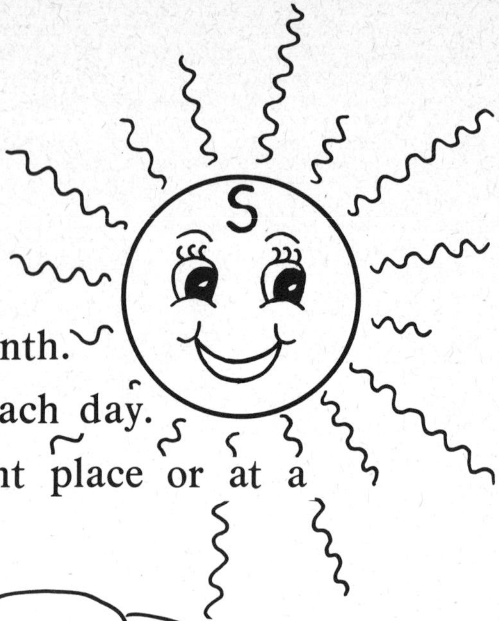

Keep a record of the temperature each day for a month.
Check the temperature at the same time and place each day.
Your partner can take the temperature at a different place or at a different time.

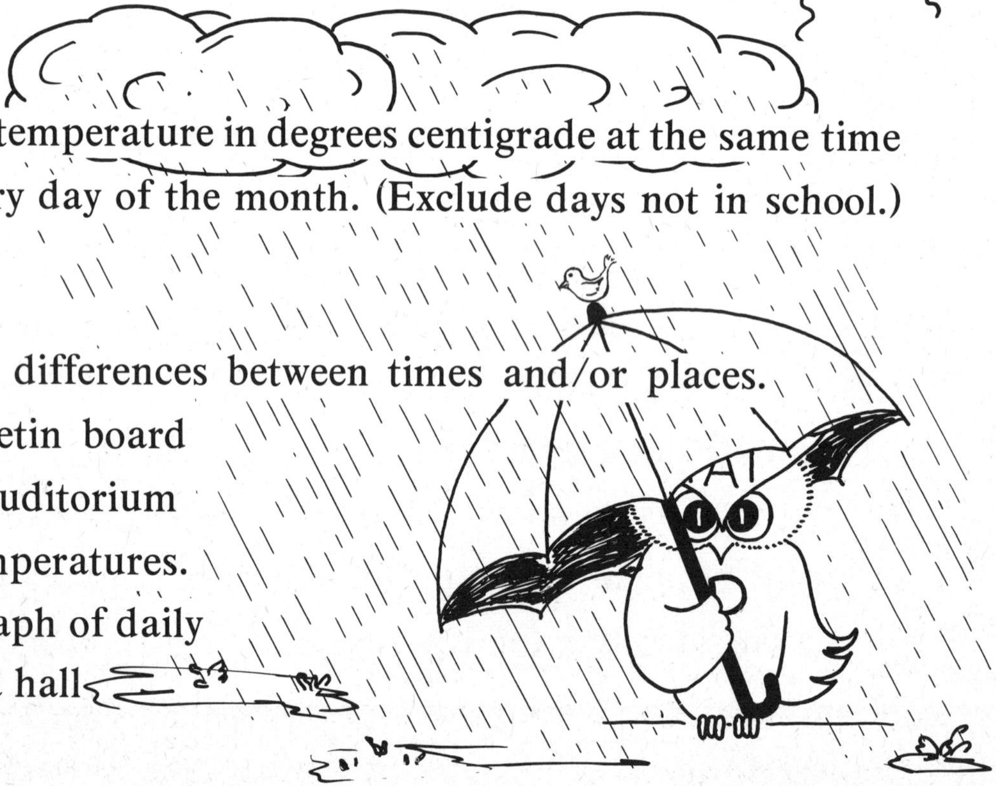

Make a graph to show temperature in degrees centigrade at the same time and place for every day of the month. (Exclude days not in school.)

Make graphs to show differences between times and/or places.

*Set up a school bulletin board in the office or auditorium to show daily temperatures.

*Keep a continuing graph of daily temperatures on a hall bulletin board.

Cool

The floor in Patrick's garage will support weight up to the weight of 1000 kiloliters of water at 4°C and 760 mm pressure.

Cool two liters of distilled water to 4°C.

Weigh a liter of the distilled water at 4°C. ____Kg

From your data compute the weight of a 1000 Kg of water at 4°C. Circle the car weights the garage floor will support.

777.3 Kg	1036.4 Kg
880 Kg	1200 Kg
980 Kg	1706.4 Kg
	1797.8 Kg

A metric ton is equivalent to 1000 Kg. Put a check after the above weights of less than a Metric Ton.

*What is the weight of your family car in Kg?

Centigrade Degrees

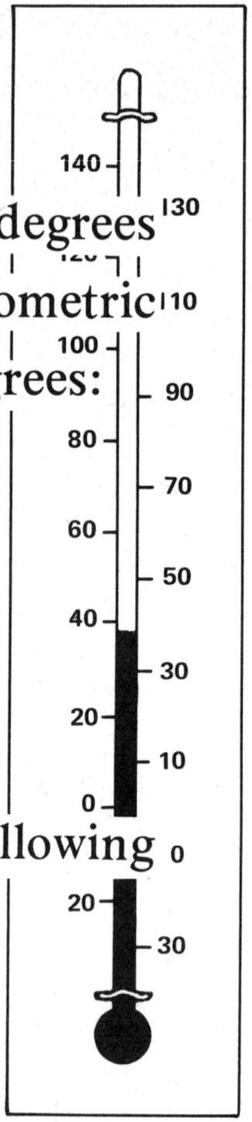

The Celsius-Centigrade thermometer has a scale of 100 degrees between the freezing and boiling points of water at 760 mm, barometric pressure at sea level. Write the temperatures in centigrade degrees:

______ °C. Boiling point of water at 760 mm pressure

______ °C. Normal body temperature

______ °C. Comfortable room temperature

______ °C. Freezing point of water at 760 mm pressure

What would you wear to school at each of the following temperatures?

____10° C. ____20° C. ____30° C. ____40° C. ____0° C.

(Write "A" for average clothes on an average day; "W" for warm clothes on a winter day; and "C" for cool clothes on a hot day.)

*What is the significance of 4°C. with regard to the Metric System?

Celsius-Centigrade

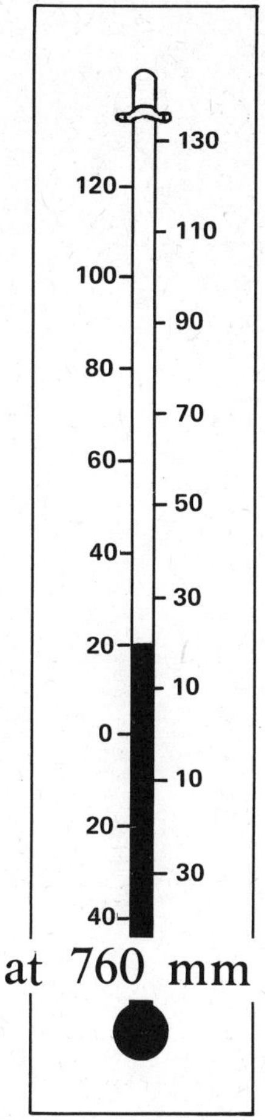

Estimate these temperatures in centrigrade degrees.

______°C. Temperature of this room

______°C. Temperature of boiling water at 760 mm

______°C. Temperature of hot water at 760 mm

______°C. Comfortable room temperature

______°C. Normal body temperature

______°C. Freezing point of water at 760 mm

______°C. Temperature of water containing Ice Melting at 760 mm

*______ °C. Temperature at which distilled water weights 1 g at 760 mm if the volume of the water is 1 cm^3

*______ °C. Temperature at which 1 liter of pure water weights 1 Kg at 760 mm

APPENDIX

Game Making Instructions and Rules

Name of the Games: *Make a Meter, Meet'er Liter, Gram Slam, Surface*

Duplicate: Six copies of each game sheet to make 48 cards for each game.
Four copies of the page of tokens will make 100 tokens, enough for a game.
The same tokens are needed for each game.

Players: From 2 to 5 players

Cards: Deck of 48 cards.

The Deal: 5 cards to each player. Cards left from dealing are placed in the center of the table and used for the stock pile. The top card of the stock pile is turned face up beside the stock pile.

Time Limit: Players should set a time limit before beginning to play.

Stock Pile Cards: During the play when the stock pile is exhausted, the discard pile is turned down (without shuffling). One card is again placed face up for the first card in the discard pile before the game continues.

Object of the Play: The object is to make one of the Standard Units (Meter, Liter, Gram). (Separate instructions for the game of Surface.) Only the most common units have been included in each deck of cards.

The Play: The player at the left of the dealer plays first, followed by the player at his left, etc.

1. Draw only one card. Draw the top card on the stock pile or the top card on the discard pile.
2. Place any number of cards with units that total a Standard Unit (Meter, Liter, Gram) face up on the table at your playing place.
3. Discard one card.

GAME RULES CONTINUED

Going Out: When a player has no more cards, he goes out and wins the deal. Play ceases and the deal is scored.

Scoring:
Make a Meter
Meet 'er Liter
Gram Slam

When a player goes out, each player gives all the cards in his hand to the winner of the deal. The winner can count only the Standard Units (Meter, Liter, Gram) that he can make with the cards that he receives from other players.

Each Standard Unit counts one point. Each player gets one point for each Standard Unit he made from his own hand and placed on the table before a player went out and won the deal.

The winner of the deal also gets a bonus of 5 points.

Surface

The rules are the same except for scoring. When a player goes out, each player gives all the cards in his hand to the winner of the deal. The winner can count centimeter squares. When a player gets 100 cenitmeter squares, he exchanges them for a decimeter square. Each player uses a different color decimeter square. Each time a player gets a decimeter square he places it on a square meter drawn on butcher paper.

Caution: The object of the game is to cover the largest area of the meter square.

1 meter square	=	100 decimeter squares
1 decimeter square	=	100 centimeter squares
1 centimeter square	=	100 millimeter squares

Keeping Scores: All players exchange points for Metric Units at the bank. The dealer is banker. He exchanges one Standard Unit for each point. When a player has collected 10 Standard Units, he must exchange them for a Deca-unit.

Score Cards: To keep his units in proper order, each player must have a score card like this:

MYRIA-	KILO-	HECTO-	HECTO-	STANDARD UNIT

Cut out these cards to play "Make a Meter." GAME INSTRUCTIONS PAGES 91 & 92.

10dm METRIC METER 10dm	10dm METRIC METER 10dm	10dm METRIC METER 10dm	1dm METRIC METER 1dm
9dm METRIC METER 9dm	9cm METRIC METER 9cm	9cm METRIC METER 9cm	1cm METRIC METER 1cm

Duplicate six copies for one game.

Cut out these cards to play "Slam Gram."

GAME INSTRUCTIONS PAGES 91 & 92.

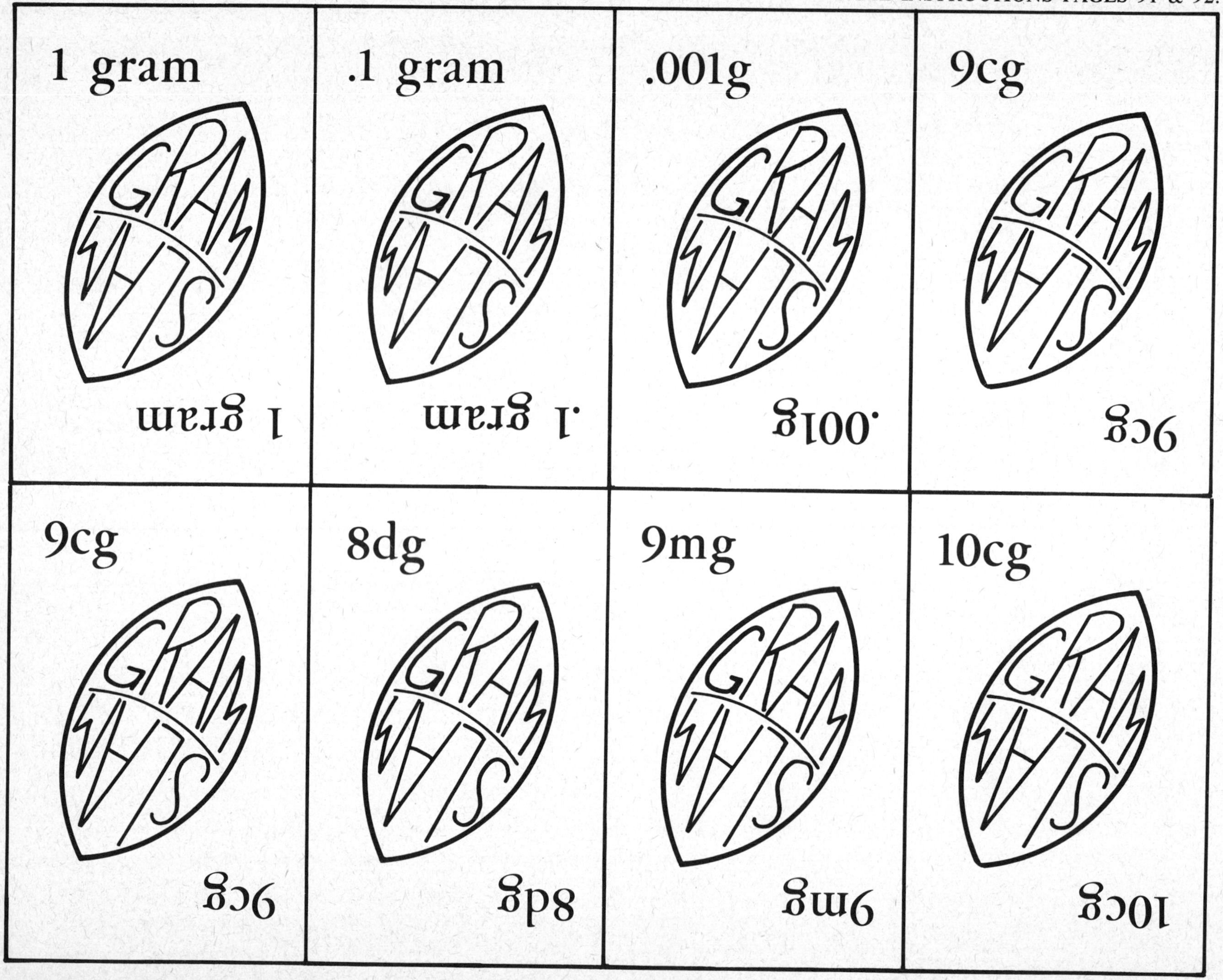

Duplicate six copies for one game.

Cut out these cards to play "Meet'er Liter."

GAME INSTRUCTIONS PAGES 91 & 92.

1000ml	5dl	300ml	100ml
10ml	50ml	400ml	9cl

Duplicate six copies for one game.

Cut out these cards to play "Surface."

GAME INSTRUCTIONS PAGES 91 & 92.

$1000cm^2$ SURFACE S SURFACE $1000cm^2$	$9dm^2$ SURFACE S SURFACE $9dm^2$	$10cm^2$ SURFACE S SURFACE $10cm^2$	$100mm^2$ SURFACE S SURFACE $100mm^2$
$9cm^2$ SURFACE S SURFACE $9cm^2$	$10mm^2$ SURFACE S SURFACE $10mm^2$	$8cm^2$ SURFACE S SURFACE $8cm^2$	$7dm^2$ SURFACE S SURFACE $7dm^2$

Duplicate six copies for one game.

Deca- Hecto- Kilo- Myria- Myria- SU SU

Deca- Hecto- SU SU

Deca- Hecto- SU SU

Game Units
Cut these out

SU stands for
Standard **U**nit

Deca- Hecto- Kilo- Deca- SU SU SU

Deca- Hecto- Kilo- Deca- SU SU SU

Four copies are needed for each game.

Estimating is Realistic

Adaptation for Mr. Joseph A. Fruwirth's ideas, which he used with pupils in the Los Angeles area.

Find pictures (Illustrations) in old magazines.

Write about a picture from your own viewpoint, but use metric units in each statement. (Look at the sample statements.)

*Find other interesting pictures and write statements about each. You may enjoy selecting pictures that best illustrate the use of one appropriate unit in each picture. For instance, illustrations of tiny objects as the leg of an insect would show an appropriate use for millimeters (mm). So would camera lenses and films. On the other hand, a picture depicting distant mountains would show the appropriate use of kilometers (km). Try to select pictures which have measurements you could check by actually measuring comparable objects, whenever someone questions the reasonableness of one of your estimations.

EXAMPLE: I am standing about 2 meters from the boat which is about ______ m long and ______ m wide. The girl is about ______ m tall and the man is about ______ m tall. The fishing pole is about ______ m long. The weight of the fish they caught is ______g. The tent is about ______m high at the lowest point. It is about ______ m long. The oar is about ______ m long. The diameter of the crown of the hat is about ______ cm long and the diameter of the brim is about ______ cm long. It is a warm day so the temperature is about ______°C.

For Teachers Only!

CONVERSION FACTORS:

1 centimeter	=	.3937 inches
1 meter	=	39.37 inches
1 kilometer	=	.6215 miles
1 liter	=	1.057 quarts
1 kilogram	=	2.205 lbs.

1 inch	=	2.560 centimeters
1 feet	=	30.48 centimeters
1 mile	=	1.609 kilometers
1 quart	=	.9461 liter
1 pound	=	453.6 grams

It's GREEK to me!

deca-	(ten)
hekto-	(hundred)
kilo-	(thousand)
myria-	(ten thousand)

GREEK prefixes are used for multiples of meter, liter, and gram.

But this is LATIN!

deci-	(tenths)
centi-	(hundredths)
milli-	(thousandths)

LATIN prefixes are used for the subunits of meter, liter, and gram.

Metric Aids

Nice to Have: Cubic Meter (Stere) Construction Kit

1. Meter stick divided into centimeters.
2. Metric ruler approximately 30 centimeters long.
3. Tape measure about 100 centimeters long.
4. Set of balances.
5. Economy scales requiring no sets of weights.
6. Capacity measures, graduated in milliliters and including one liter (1000 milliliters).
7. Bathroom scales with metric calibrations.
8. Plastic centimeter cubes.
9. Celsius-centigrade thermometer, calibrated to 110°C or 150°C.
10. cm grid transparancies.

OPTIONAL BUT NICE TO HAVE

1. Meter tape, 10, 20, 50 or 100 meters.
2. Meter rule, graduated in centimeters and millimeters.
3. Height measure, wall or free standing.
4. Self-adhesive tape with centimeters marked for converting old rulers into metric rulers and also for making graphs.
5. Plastic beakers with handles and cylinders from 10 ml to 1000 ml (liter).
6. Capacity cubes to 1 liter.
7. 5 ml spoons used by professionals in medical fields.

Sources

1. Activity Resources Company
   P. O. Box 4875
   Hayward, California 94545

2. Creative Publications
   P. O. Box 10328
   Palo Alto , California 94303

3. Cuisenaire Company of America, Inc.
   12 Church Street
   New Rochelle, New York 1085

4. "Metric-Aids" by Dick Blick
   P. O. Box 1267
   Galesburg, Illinois 61401
   (Available in West at Activity Resources Co. – See No. 1 above)

Glossary

Approximate Numbers: Reasonable but not accurate numbers. The last digit of an approximate number is reasonably correct but not exact in relation to another number.

Approximation: A problem-solving process involving a continual approach toward the exact quantity. The concept is involved in the following:

Measurement

Use of irrational numbers or rational numbers with no finite decimal representation, as pi

Use of math tables

Computing devices, as a slide rule or nomograph

Use of drawings, graphs and data used to define relation and function

Area: The measure of the surface (interior region and line) on a closed figure.

Boiling Point: Temperature at which the vapor pressure of a liquid exceeds the atmospheric pressure. At sea level (760 mm pressure) a cubic centimeter (cc) of pure water (weighing 1 gram) boils at 100° centigrade. (C-Celsius)

Capacity: A containing space.

Carat: Unit of weight (200 mg) for diamonds and other precious stones.

Centigrade: A scale, especially a temperature scale, with 100 degrees. Anders Celsius, a Swedish scientist, developed a thermometer with a scale of 100 degrees between the boiling point of water (100° C.) and the freezing point of water (0° C.) at sea level (barometric pressure 760 mm). The Celsius-centigrade thermometer is often called the centigrade thermometer.

Cube: A rectangular prism with 6 square faces.

Density: Quantity of matter per unit volume and measured by the density of water at a temperature of 4° C and with air pressure at 760 mm. The density of water, 1 gram per cubic centimeter, is the standard for measuring specific gravity. Water is also used as the standard for specific heat.

Diopter: A unit of optical power equal to one meter divided by the focal distance of a lens. Diopter powers for magnifying reading glasses include:

+1.00	+2.00	+3.00
+1.25	+2.25	+3.25
+1.50	+2.50	+3.50
+1.75	+2.75	+4.00

Edge: One of the segments making up any one of the faces of a space figure. (A cube is an example of a space figure.)

Estimate: To find the approximation for a given problem.

Exponent: The power of a number. For example: In the symbol 10^2, the 2 is the exponent indicating that 2 is the power and that 10 is used as a factor twice (10 X 10). In 10^3, the 10 is used as a factor three times: 10 X 10 X 10.

Gram: The standard unit of weight in the metric system. By definition, a gram is the weight of a cubic centimeter of water at 4° centigrade. Therefore, the gram is equal to the mass of one cubic centimeter of water at its maximum density, but is more exactly one thousandth (.001) of a standard kilogram (100 grams). A platinum weight equal to a kilogram is deposited in the Archives of State in Sevres, France near Paris. It is the standard for all metric weights. A gram is approximately 0.0352 oz.

Liter: The standard unit of capacity (volume) in the metric system. By definition the liter is a cube with edge dimension one-tenth of a meter. A liter is approximately 1.056 quarts.

Mass: The quantity of matter which a body contains, not the weight.

Meter: The standard unit of linear measurement in the metric system. By definition a meter is the wavelength of orange light emitted by krypton-86 X 1,650,763.73. This international meter is 100 times as precise as the international meter defined as the space between marks on a platinum-iridium bar kept in the Archives of State in Sevres, France near Paris. By definition, the meter was originally the distance between two marks on a platinum bar deposited in the Archives of State. It represented the best estimate in 1700 of one ten-millionth part of a terrestrial meridian that ran through Paris from the equator to the north pole. The meter is the basic unit of length and the legal international standard. It is approximately 39.37 inches.

Square: A quadrilateral with four right (square) angles and four sides of equal length.

Scientific Notation: Standard form of expressing a given number: (number between 1 and 10) X (a power of 10). For example:

Diameter of a hydrogen atom .00000001 cm as 1 X 10^{-8}

Distance to the sum: 93,000,000 miles as 9.3 X 10^7

Standard Units: Measurements defined by law. The International Committee of Weights and Measures defines and establishes each standard unit. In 1875 17 countries including the U.S. met in Sevres, France, and set up one permanent International Bureau of Weights and Measures and established:

1 International Prototype Kilogram

1 International Prototype Meter

In 1893 the U.S. Superintendent of Weights and Measures notified the state governments that the basic standards of weights and measurements in the United States would be the International Prototype Kilogram and the International Prototype Meter. He authorized the use of the Metric System by all states.

In 1901 the U.S. National Bureau of Standards defined English units of measurement in terms of the metric units.

$$1 \text{ yard} = \frac{3600}{3937} \text{ meter}$$

1 inch = 25.4 millimeters or 2.54 centimeters

1 U.S. pound = 0.4535924277 kilogram (2.2046 pounds)

1 U.S. gallon = 3,785.4 cubic centimeters (3.7854 liters)

Congress defined by law the English units of measurements in terms of the metric units and legalized the metric system in the United States. Scientists always use the metric units.

Unit: An amount of quantity defined and adopted as a standard of measurement.

Volume: Measure obtained by using a unit of the interior region of a space figure. For examples: The volume of a decimeter cube is 1 cubic decimeter which is equivalent to 1000 cubic centimeters. (The capacity is 1000 milliliters which is equivalent to 1 liter.) The volume of a centimeter cube is one cubic centimeter which is equivalent to 1000 cubic millimeters. (The capacity is 100 milliliters which is equivalent to .1 liter.) One cubic centimeter of pure water at 0°C and 760 mm pressure weighs one gram. Therefore, it is evident that all units of the metric system are related. In fact, the multiples and subdivisions of metric measures are related in a strict ratio of 1:10.

Weight: The measure of a quantity of matter (mass) balanced with a given weight. The measure of a quantity determined or measured by the amount of its downward force due to gravity. Although the mass or quantity may remain constant, a change in the pull of gravity will alter the weight as evidenced by men on the moon.

PATRICK
p

METRIC
M

SIS TIM
S

Miller, Mary
Making metric
maneuvers